ISBN 978-1-331-21627-8
PIBN 10159564

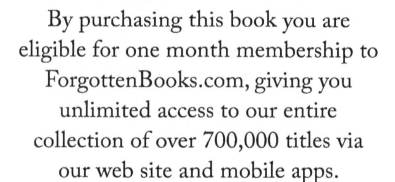

BOOK OF MORMON READY REFERENCES.

For the Use of Students and Missionaries, of the Church of Jesus Christ of Latter-day Saints.

COMPILED AND PUBLISHED BY

ELDER WILLIAM ~~A.~~ Albert MORTON, 1866-

GEO. Q. CANNON & SONS CO.

Printers.

SALT LAKE CITY, JANUARY, 1898.

PREFACE.

SEVERAL years ago Elders laboring in the British
Mission conceived the idea of compiling a small
volume of texts from the Old and New Testament,
illustrating the leading doctrines of the Church of
Jesus Christ of Latter-day Saints. The well known
little work "Ready References" was the result, a
book that has been of incalculable value to the
Elders in the various missionary fields.

It has occurred to the compiler of the present
volume that "Book of Mormon Ready References"
might be equally valuable, both to missionaries and
other Saints desirous of seeing at a glance the perfect harmony between the different sacred volumes—
"the stick of Judah" and "the stick of Ephraim."
The result is found in these pages, which are now
sent out into the world with an earnest desire that
they may help to a better understanding and appre-
ciation of the Book that came forth through the
administration of angels, and the testimony of which
has been sealed by the blood of martyrs.

The "Ready References" do not aim to make
the study of the volume itself superfluous. Their
mission is to aid that study and perhaps point the
way to a more systematic reading of the Book of
Mormon. The arrangement follows closely the

Bible "Ready References," and the plan adopted
has been favorably considered by brethren well
acquainted with the word of God, and whose
opinions, on that account, are valuable.

To the cause of God, also these References are
humbly dedicated.

WM. A. MORTON.

SALT LAKE CITY,
    Jan. 27, 1898.

CONTENTS.

BOOK OF MORMON READY REFERENCES.

For the Use of Students and Missionaries, of the Church of Jesus Christ of Latter-day Saints.

THE GOSPEL.

And it came to pass after my father had spoken these words, he spake unto my brethren concerning the Gospel which should be preached among the Jews; and also concerning the dwindling of the Jews in unbelief. And after they had slain the Messiah, who should come, and after he had been slain, he should rise from the dead, and should make himself manifest, by the Holy Ghost, unto the Gentiles.—*I. Nephi x: 11.* Spoken of by Lehi.

And now it came to pass after some years had passed away, there came a man among the people of Nephi, whose name was Sherem. Preached by Jacob.

And it came to pass that he came unto me; and on this wise did he speak unto me, saying: Brother Jacob, I have sought much opportunity that I might speak unto you: for I have heard and also know, that thou goest about much, preaching that which ye call the Gospel, or the doctrine of Christ.—*Jacob vii: 1, 6.*

For behold, I shall speak unto the Jews, and they shall write it; and I shall also speak unto the Nephites, and they All nations to have the Gospel.

All nations to have the Gospel.

shall write it; and I shall also speak unto the other tribes of the house of Israel, which I have led away, and they shall write it; and I shall also speak unto all nations of the earth, and they shall write it.

And it shall come to pass that the Jews shall have the words of the Nephites, and the Nephites shall have the words of the Jews; and the Nephites and the Jews shall have the words of the lost tribes of Israel; and the lost tribes of Israel shall have the words of the Nephites and the Jews.—II. *Nephi xxix: 12-13.*

Many parts of the Gospel taken away.

And the angel of the Lord said unto me, Thou hast beheld that the book proceeded forth from the mouth of a Jew; and when it proceeded forth from the mouth of a Jew, it contained the plainness of the Gospel of the Lord, of whom the twelve apostles bear record; and they bear record according to the truth which is in the Lamb of God;

And after they go forth by the hand of the twelve apostles of the Lamb, from the Jews unto the Gentiles, thou seest the foundation of a great and abominable church, which is most abominable above all other churches; for behold, they have taken away from the Gospel of the Lamb, many parts which are plain and most precious; and also many covenants of the Lord have they taken away.—I. *Nephi xiii: 24-26.**

---

* After the death of Christ, there was a long space of time before the gospel was put into anything like its present shape It was preached in several countries, and churches were estab-

And after these plain and precious things were taken away, it goeth forth unto all the nations of the Gentiles; and after it goeth forth unto all the nations of the Gentiles, yea even across the many waters which thou hast seen with the Gentiles which have gone forth out of captivity; thou seest because of the many plain and precious things which have been taken out of the book, which were plain unto the understanding of the children of men, according to the plainness which is in the Lamb of God; because of these things which are taken away out of the Gospel of the Lamb, an exceeding great many do stumble, yea, insomuch that Satan hath great power over them.—*I. Nephi xiii: 29.*

Causing many to stumble.

For behold thus saith Jesus Christ, the Son of God, unto his disciples who should tarry; yea, and also to all his disciples, in the hearing of the multitude, Go ye into all the world, and preach the Gospel to every creature.— *Mormon ix: 22.*

Disciples commanded to preach the Gospel.

---

lished in those countries, long before the written gospel was known much of, or, at least long before it was made use of as a guide to the Christian Churches. At the end of about four hundred years, the written gospels were laid before a council of the Catholic Church, of which the Pope was the head. But, there were several gospels besides those of Matthew, Mark, Luke, and John! Several other of the APOSTLES, or early DISCIPLES, had written gospels All these, long after the death of the authors, were, as I have just said, laid before a council of the Catholic Church; and that council determined which of the gospels were genuine and which not. It retained the four gospels of Matthew, Mark, Luke, and John; it determined that these four should be received and believed in, and that ALL THE REST SHOULD BE REJECTED.—*Cobbett's History of the Protestant Reformation, p. 9, par. 18.*

Disciples preach the Gospel.

And it came to pass that thus they did go forth among all the people of Nephi, and did preach the Gospel of Christ unto all people upon the face of the land; and they were converted unto the Lord, and were united unto the Church of Christ, and thus the people of that generation were blessed according to the words of Jesus.—*III. Nephi xxviii: 23.*

Characteristics of the Gospel.

And again I speak unto you who deny the revelations of God, and say that they are done away, that there are no more revelations, nor prophecies, nor gifts, nor healing, nor speaking with tongues, and the interpretation of tongues.

Behold I say unto you, he that denieth these things, knoweth not the Gospel of Christ; yea, he has not read the scriptures; if so, he does not understand them.—*Mormon ix: 7-8.*

Nephites deny the Gospel.

And it came to pass that when two hundred and ten years had passed away there were many churches in the land; yea, there were many churches which professed to know the Christ, and yet they did deny the more parts of his Gospel, insomuch that they did receive all manner of wickedness, and did administer that which was sacred unto him to whom it had been forbidden, because of unworthiness.—*IV. Nephi i: 27.*

Universal rejection of the Gospel.

And now, after that they have all dwindled in unbelief, and there is none, save it be the Lamanites, and they have rejected the Gospel of Christ; therefore I am commanded that I should hide them up again in the earth.—*Ether iv: 3.*

And the Lord will set his hand again the second time to restore his people from their lost and fallen state. Wherefore he will proceed to do a marvelous work and a wonder among the children of men.

Wherefore, he shall bring forth his words unto them, which words shall judge them at the last day, for they shall be given them for the purpose of convincing them of the true Messiah, who was rejected by them; and unto the convincing of them that they need not look forward any more for a Messiah to come, for there should not any come, save it should be a false Messiah, which should deceive the people: for there is save one Messiah spoken of by the prophets, and that Messiah is he who should be rejected by the Jews.—*II. Nephi xxv: 17-18.*

But behold, I prophesy unto you concerning the last days; concerning the days when the Lord God shall bring these things forth unto the children of men.

After my seed and the seed of my brethren shall have dwindled in unbelief, and shall have been smitten by the Gentiles; yea, after the Lord God shall have camped against them round about, and shall have laid siege against them with a mount, and raised forts against them; and after they shall have been brought down low in the dust, even that they are not, yet the words of the righteous shall be written, and the prayers of the faith-

The Gospel to be restored

In the last days.

ful shall be heard, and all those who have dwindled in unbelief, shall not be forgotten;

For those who shall be destroyed shall speak unto them out of the ground, and their speech shall be low out of the dust, and their voice shall be as one that hath a familiar spirit; for the Lord God will give unto him power, that he may whisper concerning them, even as it were out of the ground; and their speech shall whisper out of the dust.—*II. Nephi xxvi: 14-16.*

And now, I would prophesy somewhat more concerning the Jews and the Gentiles. For after the book of which I have spoken shall come forth, and be written unto the Gentiles, and sealed up again unto the Lord, there shall be many which shall believe the words which are written; and they shall carry them forth unto the remnant of our seed.—II. *Nephi xxx: 3.*

And the Gospel of Jesus Christ shall be declared among them; wherefore, they shall be restored unto the knowledge of their fathers, and also to the knowledge of Jesus Christ, which was had among their fathers.—*II. Nephi xxx: 5.*

And then shall the work of the Father commence at that day, even when this Gospel shall be preached among the remnant of this people. Verily I say unto you, at that day shall the work of the Father commence among all the despised of my people; yea, even the tribes which have been lost, which the Father hath led away out of Jerusalem.—III. *Nephi xxi: 26*. And the lost tribes.

And thus commandeth the Father that I should say unto you at that day when the Gentiles shall sin against my Gospel, and shall be lifted up in the pride of their hearts above all nations, and above all the people of the whole earth, and shall be filled with all manner of lyings, and of deceits, and of mischiefs, and all manner of hypocrisy and murders, and priestcrafts, and whoredoms, and of secret abominations; and if they shall do all those things, and shall reject the fulness of my Gospel, behold, saith the Father, I will bring the fulness of my Gospel from among them.—*III. Nephi xvi: 10*. To be taken from the Gentiles,

And also that ye may believe the Gospel of Jesus Christ, which ye shall have among you; and also that the Jews, the covenant people of the Lord, shall have other witnesses besides him whom they saw and heard, that Jesus whom they slew, was the very Christ, and the very God.—*Mormon iii: 21*. And given to the Jews.

Wherefore, the fruit of thy loins shall write; and the fruit of the loins of Judah shall write; and that which shall be written by the fruit of thy loins, and also that which shall be written by the fruit of the loins of Judah, shall grow together, unto the confounding of false doctrines; and laying down of contentions, and establishing peace among the

And given to the Jews.

fruit of thy loins, and bringing them to a knowledge of their fathers in the latter days; and also to a knowledge of my covenants, saith the Lord.—*II. Nephi iii: 12.*

And it shall come to pass that the Jews shall have the words of the Nephites, and the Nephites shall have the words of the Jews; and the Nephites and the Jews shall have the words of the lost tribes of Israel; and the lost tribes of Israel shall have the words of the Nephites and the Jews.—*II. Nephi xxix: 13.*

FAITH.

The First Principle of the Gospel.

Faith in God

Believe in God; believe that he is, and that he created all things, both in heaven and in earth; believe that he has all wisdom, and all power, both in heaven and in earth; believe that man doth not comprehend all the things which the Lord can comprehend.—*Mosiah iv: 9.*

But behold, I, Jacob, would speak unto you that are pure in heart. Look unto God with firmness of mind, and pray unto him with exceeding faith, and he will console you in your afflictions and he will plead your cause, and send down justice upon those who seek your destruction.—*Jacob iii: 1.*

And it came to pass that the Lord spake unto me, saying, Blessed art thou, Nephi, because of thy faith, for thou hast sought me diligently, with lowliness of heart.—*I. Nephi ii: 19.*

Nephi blessed because of his faith.

And there were many whose faith was so exceeding strong even before Christ came who could not be kept from within the vail, but truly saw with their eyes the things which they had beheld with an eye of faith, and they were glad.

Finger of God seen by faith.

And behold, we have seen in this record, that one of these was the brother of Jared: for so great was his faith in God, that when God put forth his finger, he could not hide it from the sight of the brother of Jared, because of his word which he had spoken unto him, which word he had obtained by faith.— *Ether xii: 19-20.*

And it came to pass after I, Nephi, having heard all the words of my father, concerning the things which he saw in a vision; and also the things which he spake by the power of the Holy Ghost; which power he received by faith on the Son of God; and the Son of God was the Messiah who should come; I, Nephi, was desirous, also, that I might see, and hear, and know of these things, by the power of the Holy Ghost, which is the gift of God unto all those who diligently seek him, as well in times of old as in the time that he should manifest himself unto the children of men.— *I. Nephi x: 17.*

Faith in Jesus Christ.

Faith in Jesus Christ. And when I had spoken these words, the Spirit cried with a loud voice, saying, Hosanna to the Lord, the most high God; for he is God over all the earth, yea, even above all: and blessed art thou, Nephi, because thou believest in the Son of the most high God, wherefore thou shalt behold the things which thou hast desired.—*I. Nephi xi: 6.*

Commanded to preach faith. Preach unto them repentance, and faith on the Lord Jesus Christ; teach them to humble themselves, and to be meek and lowly in heart; teach them to withstand every temptation of the devil, with their faith on the Lord Jesus Christ.—*Alma xxxvii: 33.*

Holy Ghost obtained by faith. And it came to pass after I, Nephi, having heard all the words of my father, concerning the things which he saw in a vision; and also the things which he spake by the power of the Holy Ghost; which power he received by faith on the Son of God.—*I. Nephi x: 17.*

And it came to pass that after they had spoken these words, the Spirit of the Lord came upon them, and they were filled with joy, having received a remission of their sins, and having peace of conscience, because of the exceeding faith which they had in Jesus Christ, who should come, according to the words which king Benjamin had spoken unto them.—*Mosiah iv: 3.*

And there are many among us who have
many revelations; for they are not all
stiffnecked. And as many as are not
stiffnecked and have faith, have com-
munion with the Holy Spirit, which
maketh manifest unto the children of
men, according to their faith.— *Jarom
i: 4.*

Holy Ghost
obtained by
faith.

Therefore blessed are they who humble
themselves without being compelled to
be humble; or rather, in other words,
blessed is he that believeth in the word
of God, and is baptized without stub-
bornness of heart; yea, without being
brought to know the word, or even compelled to know, before they will believe.

Faith not a
perfect
knowledge.

Yea, there are many who do say, If
thou wilt show us a sign from heaven,
then we shall know of a surety; then we
shall believe.

Now I ask is this faith? Behold, I
say unto you, nay; for if a man knoweth
a thing, he hath no cause to believe, for
he knoweth it.—*Alma xxxii: 16-18.*

And now as I said concerning faith:
Faith is not to have a perfect knowledge
of things; therefore if ye have faith, ye
hope for things which are not seen,
which are true.

And now, behold I say unto you; and
I would that ye should remember that
God is merciful unto all who believe on
his name; therefore, he desireth, in the
first place, that ye should believe, yea,
even on his word.—*Alma xxxii: 21-22.*

Can obtain every good thing by faith.

And now I come to that faith, of which I said I would speak; and I will tell you the way whereby ye may lay hold on every good thing.

And after that he came, men also were saved by faith in his name; and by faith they became the sons of God. And as sure as Christ liveth, he spake these words unto our fathers, saying, Whatsoever thing ye shall ask the Father in my name, which is good, in faith believing that ye shall receive, behold, it shall be done unto you.

And Christ hath said, If ye will have faith in me, ye shall have power to do whatsoever thing is expedient in me. — *Moroni vii: 21, 26, 33.*

Miracles wrought by faith.

Thus God has provided a means that men, through faith, might work mighty miracles; therefore he becometh a great benefit to his fellow beings.—*Mosiah viii: 18.*

And he did minister many things unto them; and all of them cannot be written, and a part of them would not suffice; therefore they are not written in this book. And Nephi did minister with power and with great authority.

And it came to pass that they were angry with him, even because he had greater power than they, for it were not possible that they could disbelieve his words, for so great was his faith on the Lord Jesus Christ, that angels did minister unto him daily;

And in the name of Jesus did he cast out devils and unclean spirits; and even his brother did he raise from the dead, after he had been stoned and suffered death by the people;

By faith Nephi raises the dead.

And the people saw it, and did witness of it, and were angry with him, because of his power; and he did also do many more miracles, in the sight of the people, in the name of Jesus.—III. *Nephi vii: 17-20.*

And there were great and marvelous works wrought by the disciples of Jesus, insomuch that they did heal the sick, and raise the dead, and cause the lame to walk, and the blind to receive sight, and the deaf to hear; and all manner of miracles did they work among the children of men; and in nothing did they work miracles save it were in the name of Jesus.—*IV. Nephi i: 5.*

Miracles wrought by the disciples.

Now, behold, there were two thousand of these young men who entered into this covenant, and took their weapons of war to defend their country.

By faith two thousand young men are saved in battle.

And they were all young men, and they were exceeding valiant for courage, and also for strength and activity; but behold this was not all: they were men who were true at all times in whatsoever thing they were entrusted;

Yea, they were men of truth and soberness, for they had been taught to keep the commandments of God, and to walk uprightly before him.—*Alma liii: 18, 20-21.*

By faith two thousand young men are saved in battle.

But behold, my little band of two thousand and sixty, fought most desperately; yea, they were firm before the Lamanites, and did administer death unto all those who opposed them;

Yea, and they did obey and observe to perform every word of command with exactness; yea, and even according to their faith it was done unto them; and I did remember the words which they said unto me, that their mothers had taught them.

And it came to pass that there were two hundred, out of my two thousand and sixty, who had fainted because of the loss of blood; nevertheless, according to the goodness of God, and to our great astonishment, and also the foes of our whole army, there was not one soul of them who did perish; yea, and neither was there one soul among them who had not received many wounds.

And now, their preservation was astonishing to our whole army; yea, that they should be spared, while there was a thousand of our brethren who were slain. And we do justly ascribe it to the miraculous power of God, because of their exceeding faith in that which they had been taught to believe, that there was a just God; and whosoever did not doubt, that they should be preserved by his marvelous power.—*Alma lvii: 19, 21, 25-26.*

FAITH AND WORKS.

For I command all men, both in the east and in the west, and in the north, and in the south, and in the islands of the sea, that they shall write the words which I speak unto them: for out of the books which shall be written I will judge the world, every man according to their works, according to that which is written.—II. *Nephi xxix: 11.*

Every soul to be judged according to his works.

And these things do the Spirit manifest unto me; therefore I write unto you all. And for this cause I write unto you, that ye may know that ye must all stand before the judgment seat of Christ, yea, every soul who belongs to the whole human family of Adam; and ye must stand to be judged of your works, whether they be good or evil.—*Mormon iii: 20.*

Wherefore if they should die in their wickedness, they must be cast off, also, as to the things which are spiritual, which are pertaining to righteousness; wherefore, they must be brought to stand before God, to be judged of their works; and if their works have been filthiness, they must needs be filthy; and if they be filthy, it must needs be that they cannot dwell in the kingdom of God: if so, the kingdom of God must be filthy also.— *I. Nephi xv: 33.*

Words of
Mosiah.

Therefore, I would that you should be steadfast and immovable, always abounding in good works, that Christ, the Lord God Omnipotent, may seal you his, that you may be brought to heaven, that ye may have everlasting salvation and eternal life, through the wisdom, and power, and justice, and mercy of him, who created all things, in heaven and in earth, who is God above all. Amen.—*Mosiah v: 15.*

Words of
Alma.

And now, my son, remember the words which I have spoken unto you; trust not those secret plans unto this people, but teach them an everlasting hatred against sin and iniquity;

Preach unto them repentance, and faith on the Lord Jesus Christ; teach them to humble themselves, and to be meek and lowly in heart; teach them to withstand every temptation of the devil, with their faith on the Lord Jesus Christ;

Teach them never to be weary of good works, but to be meek and lowly in heart; for such shall find rest to their souls.—*Alma xxxvii: 32-34.*

And it is requisite with the justice of God, that men should be judged according to their works; and if their works were good in this life, and the desires of their hearts were good, that they should also, at the last day, be restored unto that which is good;

And if their works are evil, they shall be restored unto him for evil; therefore, all things shall be restored to their proper order; everything to its natural frame; mortality raised to immortality; corruption to incorruption; raised to endless happiness, to inherit the kingdom of God, or to endless misery, to inherit the kingdom of the devil, the one on one hand, the other on the other;

Words of Alma.

The one raised to happiness according to his desires of happiness; or good, according to his desires of good; and the other evil according to his desires of evil; for as he has desired to do evil all the day long, even so shall he have his reward of evil when the night cometh.— *Alma xli: 3-5.*

Therefore prepare ye the way of the Lord, for the time is at hand that all men shall reap a reward of their works, according to that which they have been: if they have been righteous, they shall reap the salvation of their souls, according to the power and deliverance of Jesus Christ: and if they have been evil, they shall reap the damnation of their souls, according to the power and captivation of the devil.—*Alma ix: 28.*

Rewarded according to our works.

And now, may the peace of God rest upon you, and upon your houses and lands, and upon your flocks and herds, and all that you possess; your women and your children, according to your faith and good works, from this time forth and for ever. And thus I have spoken. Amen.—*Alma vii: 27.*

Prayer of Alma.

REPENTANCE.

Repentance preached by prophets at Jerusalem.

For it came to pass in the commencement of the first year of the reign of Zedekiah, King of Judah (my father Lehi, having dwelt in Jerusalem in all his days); and in that same year there came many prophets, prophesying unto the people that they must repent, or the great city Jerusalem must be destroyed.—*I. Nephi i: 4.*

Words spoken by an angel.

And it came to pass that the angel spake unto me, Nephi, saying, 'Thou hast beheld that if the Gentiles repent, it shall be well with them; and thou also knowest concerning the covenants of the Lord unto the house of Israel; and thou also hast heard, that whoso repenteth not, must perish.—*I. Nephi xiv: 5.*

Repentance preached by Alma.

Yea, thus saith the Spirit, Repent, all ye ends of the earth, for the kingdom of heaven is soon at hand; yea, the Son of God cometh in his glory, in his might, majesty, power, and dominion. Yea, my beloved brethren, I say unto you, that the Spirit saith, Behold the glory of the King of all the earth; and also the King of heaven shall very soon shine forth among all the children of men;

And also the Spirit saith unto me, yea, crieth unto me with a mighty voice, saying, Go forth and say unto this people, Repent, for except ye repent ye can in no wise inherit the kingdom of heaven.—*Alma v: 50-51.*

Now I say unto you, that ye must repent, and be born again: for the Spirit saith, If ye are not born again, ye cannot inherit the kingdom of heaven; therefore come and be baptized unto repentance, that ye may be washed from your sins, that ye may have faith on the Lamb of God, who taketh away the sins of the world, who is mighty to save and to cleanse from all unrighteousness;

Yea, I say unto you, come and fear not, and lay aside every sin, which easily doth beset you, which doth bind you down to destruction, yea, come and go forth, and shew unto your God that ye are willing to repent of your sins, and enter into a covenant with him to keep his commandments, and witness it unto him this day, by going into the waters of baptism.—*Alma vii: 14-15.*

Repentance preached by Alma.

And the days of the children of men were prolonged, according to the will of God, that they might repent while in the flesh; wherefore, their state became a state of probation, and their time was lengthened, according to the commandments which the Lord God gave unto the children of men. For he gave commandment that all men must repent; for he shewed unto all men that they were lost, because of the transgression of their parents.—II. *Nephi ii: 21.*

Men's days prolonged that they might repent

And we see that death comes upon mankind, yea, the death which has been spoken of by Amulek, which is the temporal death; nevertheless there was a space granted unto man in which he

Should repent in this life.

might repent; therefore this life became a probationary state; a time to prepare to meet God; a time to prepare for that endless state which has been spoken of by us, which is after the resurrection of the dead.—*Alma xii: 24.*

Should not procrastinate the day of repentance.

For behold, this life is the time for men to prepare to meet God; yea, behold the day of this life is the day for men to perform their labors.

And now as I said unto you before, as ye have had so many witnesses, therefore, I beseech of you, that you do not procrastinate the day of your repentance until the end; for after this day of life, which is given us to prepare for eternity, behold, if we do not improve our time while in this life, then cometh the night of darkness, wherein there can be no labor performed.

Ye cannot say, when ye are brought to that awful crisis, that I will repent, that I will return to my God. Nay, ye cannot say this; for that same spirit which doth possess your bodies at the time that ye go out of this life, that same spirit will have power to possess your body in that eternal world.

For behold, if ye have procrastinated the day of your repentance, even until death; behold, ye have become subjected to the spirit of the devil, and he doth seal you his; therefore, the Spirit of the Lord hath withdrawn from you, and hath no place in you, and hath all power over you; and this is the final state of the wicked.—*Alma xxxiv: 32-35.*

But woe unto him that has the law given; yea, that has all the commandments of God, like unto us, and that transgresseth them, and that wasteth the days of his probation, for awful is his state.—II. *Nephi ix: 27.*

Should not procrastinate the day of repentance.

Hath he commanded any that they should not partake of his salvation? Behold I say unto you, Nay; but he hath given it free for all men; and he hath commanded his people that they should persuade all men to repentance. — II. *Nephi xxvi: 27.*

All men commanded to repent.

And he commandeth all men that they must repent, and be baptized in his name, having perfect faith in the Holy One of Israel, or they cannot be saved in the kingdom of God. —II. *Nephi ix: 23.*

For he is the same yesterday, to-day, and for ever; and the way is prepared for all men from the foundation of the world, if it so be that they repent and come unto him.—*I. Nephi x: 18.*

Yea, he that repenteth and exerciseth faith, and bringeth forth good works, and prayeth continually without ceasing: unto such it is given to know the mysteries of God; yea, unto such it shall be given to reveal things which never have been revealed; yea, and it shall be given unto such to bring thousands of souls to repentance, even as it has been given unto us to bring these our brethren to repentance.—*Alma xxvi: 22.*

Blessings to be obtained by repentance.

Invitation of Jesus.

Therefore, repent all ye ends of the earth, and come unto me, and believe in my gospel, and be baptized in my name; for he that believeth, and is baptized, shall be saved; but he that believeth not, shall be damned; and signs shall follow them that believe in my name.— *Ether iv: 18.*

WATER BAPTISM.

But one baptism.

And he commanded them that there should be no contention one with another, but that they should look forward with one eye, having one faith and one baptism; having their hearts knit together in unity and in love, one towards another.—*Mosiah xviii: 21.*

Baptism of Jesus.

And now, if the Lamb of God, he being holy, should have need to be baptized by water, to fulfil all righteousness, O then, how much more need have we, being unholy, to be baptized, yea, even by water.

And now, I would ask of you, my beloved brethren, wherein the Lamb of God did fulfil all righteousness in being baptized by water?

Know ye not that he was holy? But notwithstanding he being holy, he sheweth unto the children of men, that according to the flesh, he humbleth himself before the Father, and witnesseth unto the Father that he would be obedient unto him in keeping his commandments.—II. *Nephi xxxi: 5-7.*

And the Father said, Repent ye, repent ye, and be baptized in the name of my beloved Son.

And also, the voice of the Son came unto me, saying, He that is baptized in my name, to him will the Father give the Holy Ghost, like unto me; wherefore, follow me, and do the things which ye have seen me do.—*II. Nephi xxxi: 11-12.*

Baptism commanded of God.

And he commandeth all men that they must repent, and be baptized in his name, having perfect faith in the Holy One of Israel, or they cannot be saved in the kingdom of God.—*II. Nephi ix: 23.*

MODE OF BAPTISM.

And again the Lord called others, and said unto them likewise; and he gave unto them power to baptize. And he said unto them, On this wise shall ye baptize; and there shall be no disputations among you.

Proofs in favor of immersion.

Verily I say unto you, that whoso repenteth of his sins through your words, and desireth to be baptized in my name, on this wise shall ye baptize them: behold ye shall go down and stand in the water, and in my name shall ye baptize them.

And now behold, these are the words

which ye shall say, calling them by name,
saying,

Having authority given me of Jesus
Christ, I baptize you in the name of the
Father, and of the Son, and of the Holy
Ghost.   Amen.

And then shall ye immerse them in
the water, and come forth again out of
the water.—*III. Nephi xi: 22-26.*

And now it came to pass that Alma
took Helam, he being one of the first,
and went and stood forth in the water,
and cried, saying, O Lord, pour out thy
Spirit upon thy servant, that he may do
this work with holiness of heart.

And when he had said these words,
the Spirit of the Lord was upon him,
and he said, Helam, I baptize thee,
having authority from the Almighty God,
as a testimony that ye have entered into
a covenant to serve him until you are
dead, as to the mortal body; and may
the Spirit of the Lord be poured out
upon you; and may he grant unto you
eternal life, through the redemption of
Christ, whom he has prepared from the
foundation of the world.

And after Alma had said these words,
both Alma and Helam were buried in the
water; and they arose and came forth
out of the water rejoicing, being filled
with the Spirit.

And again, Alma took another, and
went forth a second time into the water,
and baptized him according to the first,
only he did not bury himself again in
the water.

And after this manner he did baptize Proofs in every one that went forth to the place of favor of im- Mormon: and they were in number about mersion. two hundred and four souls; yea, and they were baptized in the waters of Mormon, and were filled with the grace of God.—*Mosiah xviii: 12-16.*

And it came to pass that Nephi went down into the water, and was baptized.

And he came up out of the water and began to baptize. And he baptized all those whom Jesus had chosen.

And it came to pass when they were all baptized, and had come up out of the water, the Holy Ghost did fall upon them, and they were filled with the Holy Ghost, and with fire.—III. *Nephi xix: 11-13.*

OBJECT OF BAPTISM.

Now, I say unto you, that ye must re- For the pent, and be born again: for the Spirit remission of saith, If ye are not born again, ye can- sins. not inherit the kingdom of heaven; therefore come and be baptized unto repentance, that ye may be washed from your sins, that ye may have faith on the Lamb of God, who taketh away the sins of the world, who is mighty to save and to cleanse from all unrighteousness. — *Alma vii: 14.*

And again, more blessed are they who shall believe in your words, because that ye shall testify that ye have seen me, and that ye know that I am. Yea, blessed are they who shall believe in your words,

For the
remission of
sins.

and come down into the depths of
humility and be baptized, for they shall
be visited with fire and with the Holy
Ghost, and shall receive a remission of
their sins.—III. *Nephi xii: 2.*

And it came to pass that Nephi went
forth among the people, and also many
others, baptizing unto repentance, in the
which there were a great remission of
sins.　And thus the people began again
to have peace in the land.—*III. Nephi
i: 23.*

Turn, all ye Gentiles from your wicked
ways, and repent of your evil doings, of
your lyings and deceivings, and of your
whoredoms, and of your secret abominations, and your idolatries, and of your
murders, and your priestcrafts, and your
envyings, and your strifes, and from all
your wickedness and abominations, and
come unto me, and be baptized in my
name, that ye may receive a remission
of your sins, and be filled with the Holy
Ghost, that ye may be numbered with
my people, who are of the house of
Israel.—III. *Nephi xxx: 2.*

PROPER SUBJECTS FOR BAPTISM.

Baptism
of little
children for-
bidden.

Listen to the words of Christ, your
Redeemer, your Lord and your God.
Behold, I came into the world not to call
the righteous, but sinners to repentance:
the whole need no physician, but they
that are sick; wherefore little children
are whole, for they are not capable of
committing sin; wherefore the curse of

Adam is taken from them in me, that it hath no power over them; and the law of circumcision is done away in me.

And after this manner did the Holy Ghost manifest the word of God unto me; wherefore my beloved son, I know that it is solemn mockery before God, that ye should baptize little children.

Behold I say unto you, That this thing shall ye teach, repentance and baptism unto those who are accountable and capable of committing sin; yea, teach parents that they must repent and be baptized, and humble themselves as their little children, and they shall all be saved with their little children.

And their little children need no repentance, neither baptism. Behold, baptism is unto repentance to the fulfilling the commandments unto the remission of sins.

But little children are alive in Christ, even from the foundation of the world; if not so, God is a partial God, and also a changeable God, and a respecter to persons; for how many little children have died without baptism.

Wherefore, if little children could not be saved without baptism, these must have gone to an endless hell.

Behold, I say unto you, That he that supposeth that little children need baptism, is in the gall of bitterness, and in the bonds of iniquity; for he hath neither faith, hope, nor charity; wherefore, should he be cut off while in the thought, he must go down to hell.—*Moroni viii: 8-14.*

Must be
capable of
being taught,

And it came to 'pass that after Alma had taught the people many things, and had made an end of speaking to them, that king Limhi was desirous that he might be baptized; and all his people were desirous that they might be baptized also.—*Mosiah xxv: 17.*

And of
believing,

And it came to pass that there were many that did believe in their words; and as many as did believe, were baptized; and they became a righteous people, and they did establish a church among them.—*Alma xix: 35.*

And of
repenting.

And it came to pass that whosoever did not belong to the church who repented of their sins, were baptized unto repentance, and were received into the church.—*Alma vi: 2.*

THE HOLY GHOST.

Promised by
Messiah.

And also, the voice of the Son came unto me, saying, He that is baptized in my name, to him will the Father give the Holy Ghost, like unto me; wherefore, follow me, and do the things which ye have seen me do.—II. *Nephi xxxi: 12.*

And ye shall offer for a sacrifice unto me a broken heart and a contrite spirit. And whoso cometh unto me with a broken heart and a contrite spirit, him will I baptize with fire and with the Holy Ghost, even as the Lamanites, because of their faith in me at the time of their conversion, were baptized with fire and with the Holy Ghost, and they knew it not.—*III. Nephi ix: 20.*

Wherefore, my beloved brethren, I know that if ye shall follow the Son, with full purpose of heart, acting no hypocrisy and no deception before God, but with real intent, repenting of your sins, witnessing unto the Father, that ye are willing to take upon you the name of Christ, by baptism: yea, by following your Lord and your Savior down into the water, according to his word; behold, then shall ye receive the Holy Ghost; yea, then cometh the baptism of fire and of the Holy Ghost; and then can ye speak with the tongue of angels, and shout praises unto the Holy One of Israel.—*II. Nephi xxxi: 13.* *Promised by Nephi.*

And it came to pass after I had seen the tree, I said unto the Spirit, I behold thou hast shewn unto me the tree which is precious above all. *The Holy Ghost a personage of spirit.*

And he said unto me, What desirest thou?

And I said unto him, to know the interpretation thereof; for I spake unto him as a man speaketh; for I beheld that he was in the form of a man; yet nevertheless I knew that it was the Spirit of the Lord; and he spake unto me as a man speaketh with another.*—*I. Nephi xi: 9-11.*

---

* The Holy Ghost has not a body of flesh and bones, but is a *personage* of spirit.—JOSEPH SMITH.

GIFTS OF THE SPIRIT.

Gift of tongues.

Do ye not remember that I said unto you, That after ye had received the Holy Ghost, ye could speak with the tongue of angels? And now, how could ye speak with the tongue of angels, save it were by the Holy Ghost?—*II. Nephi xxxii: 2.*

Gift of prophecy.

And Alma went forth, and also Amulek, among the people, to declare the words of God unto them; and they were filled with the Holy Ghost;

And it came to pass that they went forth and began to preach and to prophesy unto the people, according to the Spirit and power which the Lord had given them.—*Alma viii: 30, 32.*

Gift of revelation, of preaching, and of translation.

Having been visited by the Spirit of God; having conversed with angels, and having been spoken unto by the voice of the Lord; and having the Spirit of prophecy, and the Spirit of revelation, and also many gifts: the gift of speaking with tongues, and the gift of preaching, and the gift of the Holy Ghost, and the gift of translation.—*Alma ix: 21.*

Visions.

And it came to pass after I, Nephi, having heard all the words of my father, concerning the things which he saw in a vision; and also the things which he spake by the power of the Holy Ghost; which power he received by faith on the Son of God; and the Son of God was the Messiah who should come; I, Nephi, was desirous also, that I might see, and hear, and know of these things, by the power of the Holy Ghost, which is the gift of God unto all those who diligently seek him, as well in times of old as in the time that he should manifest himself unto the children of men.—*I. Nephi x: 17.*

And also Zeezrom lay sick at Sidom, with a burning fever, which was caused by the great tribulations of his mind, on account of his wickedness, for he supposed that Alma and Amulek were no more; and he supposed that they had been slain, by the cause of his iniquity. And this great sin, and his many other sins, did harrow up his mind until it did become exceeding sore, having no deliverance; therefore he began to be scorched with a burning heat.

Gift of healing.

Now when he heard that Alma and Amulek were in the land of Sidom, his heart began to take courage; and he sent a message immediately unto them, desiring them to come unto him.

And then Alma cried unto the Lord, saying, O Lord our God, have mercy on this man, and heal him according to his faith which is in Christ.

And when Alma had said these words, Zeezrom leaped upon his feet, and began to walk; and this was done to the great astonishment of all the people; and the knowledge of this went forth throughout all the land of Sidom.—*Alma xv: 3-4, 10-11.*

And in the name of Jesus did he cast out devils and unclean spirits; and even his brother did he raise from the dead, after he had been stoned and suffered death by the people.—*III. Nephi vii: 19.*

Spiritual
gifts.

For behold thus saith Jesus Christ, the Son of God, unto his disciples who should tarry; yea, and also to all his disciples, in the hearing of the multitude, Go ye into all the world, and preach the gospel to every creature,

And he that believeth and is baptized, shall be saved, and he that believeth not, shall be damned.

And these signs shall follow them that believe; in my name shall they cast out devils; they shall speak with new tongues; they shall take up serpents; and if they drink any deadly thing, it shall not hurt them; they shall lay hands on the sick and they shall recover. — *Mormon ix: 22-24.*

And again I exhort you, my brethren, that ye deny not the gifts of God, for they are many; and they come from the same God. And there are different ways that these gifts are administered; but it is the same God who worketh all in all; and they are given by the manifestations of the Spirit of God unto men, to profit them.

For behold, to one is given by the Spirit of God, that he may teach the word of wisdom;

And to another, that he may teach the word of knowledge by the same Spirit;

And to another, exceeding great faith; and to another, the gift of healing by the same Spirit.

And again, to another, that he may work mighty miracles;

And again, to another that he may prophesy concerning all things;

And again, to another, the beholding of angels and ministering spirits;

And again, to another, all kinds of tongues;

And again, to another, the interpretation of languages and of divers kinds of tongues.

And all these gifts come by the Spirit of Christ; and they come unto every man severally, according as he will.—*Moroni x: 8-17.*

LAYING ON OF HANDS TO CONFER THE HOLY GHOST.

Now it came to pass that when Alma had said these words, that he clapped his hands upon all them who were with him. And behold, as he clapped his hands upon them they were filled with the Holy Spirit.—*Alma xxxi: 36.* Holy Ghost conferred by the laying on of hands.

And it came to pass that when Jesus had made an end of these sayings, he touched with his hand the disciples whom he had chosen, one by one, even until he had touched them all, and spake unto them as he touched them;

And the multitude heard not the words which he spake, therefore they did not bear record; but the disciples bear record that he gave them power to give the Holy Ghost. And I will shew unto you hereafter that this record is true.—*III. Nephi xviii: 36-37.*

The words of Christ, which he spake unto his disciples, the twelve whom he had chosen, as he laid his hands upon them.

And he called them by name, saying, Ye shall call on the Father, in my name, in mighty prayer; and after ye have done this, ye shall have power that on him whom ye shall lay your hands, ye shall give the Holy Ghost; and in my name shall ye give it, for thus do mine apostles.

Now Christ spake these words unto them at the time of his first appearing; and the multitude heard it not, but the disciples heard it; and on as many as they laid their hands, fell the Holy Ghost.—*Moroni ii: 1-3.*

THE SACRAMENT OF THE LORD'S SUPPER.

Instituted by Jesus.   And it came to pass that Jesus commanded his disciples that they should bring forth some bread and wine unto him.

And while they were gone for bread and wine, he commanded the multitude that they should sit themselves down upon the earth.

And when the disciples had come with bread and wine, he took of the bread, and brake and blessed it; and he gave unto the disciples, and commanded that they should eat.

And when they had eat, and were filled, he commanded that they should give unto the multitude.

And when the multitude had eaten and were filled, he said unto the disciples, behold there shall one be ordained among you, and to him will I give power that he shall break bread, and bless it, and give it unto the people of my church, unto all those who shall believe and be baptized in my name. *For members of the Church only.*

And this shall ye always observe to do, even as I have done, even as I have broken bread, and blessed it, and gave it unto you.

And this shall ye do in remembrance of my body, which I have shewn unto you. And it shall be a testimony unto the Father, that ye do always remember me. And if ye do always remember me, ye shall have my Spirit to be with you. *The bread an emblem of Christ's body.*

And it came to pass that when he said these words, he commanded his disciples that they should take of the wine of the cup, and drink of it, and that they should also give unto the multitude, that they might drink of it.

And it came to pass that they did so, and did drink of it, and were filled; and they gave unto the multitude, and they did drink, and they were filled.

And when the disciples had done this Jesus said unto them, Blessed are ye for this thing which ye have done, for this is fulfilling my commandments, and this doth witness unto the Father that ye are willing to do that which I have commanded you.

And this shall ye always do to those who repent and are baptized in my name;

The wine an emblem of Christ's blood.

and ye shall do it in remembrance of my blood, which I have shed for you, that ye may witness unto the Father that ye do always remember me. And if ye do always remember me, ye shall have my Spirit to be with you.

And I give unto you a commandment that ye shall do these things. And if ye shall always do these things, blessed are ye, for ye are built upon my rock.—*III. Nephi xviii: 1-12.*

Christ administers the Sacrament the second time.

And it came to pass that he brake bread again, and blessed it, and gave to the disciples to eat.

And when they had eaten, he commanded them that they should break bread, and give it unto the multitude.

And when they had given unto the multitude, he also gave them wine to drink, and commanded them that they should give unto the multitude.

And he said unto them, he that eateth this bread, eateth of my body to his soul, and he that drinketh of this wine, drinketh of my blood to his soul, and his soul shall never hunger nor thirst, but shall be filled.— III. *Nephi xx: 3-5, 8.*

Manner of administering the Sacrament.

The manner of their Elders and Priests administering the flesh and blood of Christ unto the church. And they administered it according to the commandments of Christ; wherefore we know the manner to be true; and the Elder or Priest did minister it.

And they did kneel down with the

church, and pray to the Father in the name of Christ, saying,

O God, the Eternal Father, we ask thee in the name of thy Son Jesus Christ, to bless and sanctify this bread to the souls of all those who partake of it, that they may eat in remembrance of the body of thy Son, and witness unto thee, O God, the Eternal Father, that they are willing to take upon them the name of thy Son, and always remember him, and keep his commandments which he hath given them, that they may always have his Spirit to be with them. Amen.— *Moroni iv: 1-3.*

The manner of administering the wine. Behold, they took the cup, and said,

O God, the Eternal Father, we ask thee, in the name of thy Son, Jesus Christ, to bless and sanctify this wine to the souls of all those who drink of it, that they may do it in remembrance of the blood of thy Son, which was shed for them, that they may witness unto thee, O God, the Eternal Father, that they do always remember him, that they may have his Spirit to be with them. Amen.—*Moroni v: 1-2.*

Manner of administering the Sacrament.

Behold verily, verily I say unto you, I give unto you another commandment, and then I must go unto my Father, that I may fulfil other commandments which he hath given me.

And now behold, this is the commandment which I give unto you, that ye shall not suffer any one knowingly, to

Not to be partaken of unworthily.

partake of my flesh and blood unworthily. when ye shall minister it;

For whoso eateth and drinketh my
flesh and blood unworthily, eateth and
drinketh damnation to his soul; therefore if ye know that a man is unworthy
to eat and drink of my flesh and blood, ye
shall forbid him.—*III. Nephi xviii: 27-29.*

Not to be
partaken of
unworthily.

See that ye are not baptized unworthily; see that ye partake not of the sacrament of Christ unworthily; but see that
ye do all things in worthiness, and do it
in the name of Jesus Christ, the Son of
the living God; and if ye do this, and
endure to the end, ye will in no wise be
cast out.—*Mormon ix: 29.*

MARRIAGE.

Marriage
commanded
of God.

And now I would that ye might know,
that after my father, Lehi, had made an
end of prophesying concerning his seed,
it came to pass that the Lord spake unto
him again, saying, that it was not meet
for him, Lehi, that he should take his
family into the wilderness alone; but
that his sons should take daughters to
wife, that they might raise up seed unto
the Lord in the land of promise.

And it came to pass that the Lord
commanded him that I, Nephi, and my
brethren, should again return unto the

land of Jerusalem, and bring down Ishmael and his family into the wilderness.— I. *Nephi vii: 1-2.*

And it came to pass that I, Nephi, took one of the daughters of Ishmael to wife; and also, my brethren took of the daughters of Ishmael to wife; and also Zoram took the eldest daughter of Ishmael to wife.

Marriage commanded of God.

And thus my father had fulfilled all the commandments of the Lord which had been given unto him. And also, I, Nephi, had been blessed of the Lord exceedingly.—*I. Nephi xvi: 7-8.*

Wherefore, my brethren, hear me, and hearken to the word of the Lord; for there shall not any man among you have save it be one wife; and concubines he shall have none.

For if I will saith the Lord of Hosts, raise up seed unto me, I will command my people; otherwise they shall hearken unto these things.—*Jacob ii, 27, 30.*

And it came to pass that after Mosiah had done as his father had commanded him, and had made a proclamation throughout all the land, that the people gathered themselves together throughout all the land, that they might go up to the temple to hear the words which king Benjamin should speak unto them.

Marriage among the Nephites

And it came to pass that when they came up to the temple, they pitched their tents round about, every man according to his family, consisting of his

wife, and his sons, and his daughters
and their sons, and their daughters, from
the eldest down to the youngest, every
family being separate one from another.—
Mosiah ii: 1, 5.

Marriage   And it came to pass that he commanded
among   that their little children should be
the Nephites brought.

So they brought their little children
and sat them down upon the ground
round about him, and Jesus stood in the
midst; and the multitude gave way till
they had all been brought unto him.

And he spake unto the multitude, and
saith unto them, behold your little ones.

And as they looked to behold, they
cast their eyes towards heaven, and they
saw the heavens open, and they saw
angels descending out of heaven as it
were, in the midst of fire; and they came
down and encircled those little ones
about, and they were encircled about
with fire; and the angels did minister
unto them,

And the multitude did see and hear
and bear record; and they know that
their record is true for they all of them
did see and hear, every man for himself;
and they were in number about two
thousand and five hundred souls; and
they did consist of men, women, and
children.—III. *Nephi xvii: 11-12, 23-25.*

DIVINE AUTHORITY.

For behold it came to pass that the Lord spake unto my father, yea, even in a dream, and said unto him, Blessed art thou Lehi, because of the things which thou hast done; and because thou hast been faithful and declared unto this people the things which I commanded thee, behold they seek to take away thy life.—*I. Nephi ii: 1.*

Lehi called of God.

And it came to pass that the Lord spake unto me, saying, Blessed art thou, Nephi, because of thy faith, for thou hast sought me diligently, with lowliness of heart.

And inasmuch as thou shalt keep my commandments, thou shalt be made a ruler and a teacher over thy brethren.—*I. Nephi ii: 19, 22.*

Nephi called and chosen to be a ruler and teacher.

And it came to pass as they smote us with a rod, behold an angel of the Lord came and stood before them, and he spake unto them, saying, Why do ye smite your younger brother with a rod? Know ye not that the Lord hath chosen him to be a ruler over you, and this because of your iniquities? Behold ye shall go up to Jerusalem again, and the Lord will deliver Laban into your hands.—*I. Nephi iii: 29.*

And behold, the words of the Lord had been fulfilled unto my brethren, which he spake concerning them, that I should be their ruler and their teacher; wherefore, I had been their ruler and their teacher, according to the commandments of the Lord, until the time they sought to take away my life.—*II. Nephi v: 19.*

Nephi consecrates Priests and Teachers.

And it came to pass that I, Nephi, did consecrate Jacob and Joseph, that they should be priests and teachers over the land of my people.—*II. Nephi v: 26.*

Behold, my beloved brethren, I, Jacob, having been called of God, and ordained after the manner of his holy order, and having been consecrated by my brother Nephi, unto whom ye look as a king or a protector, and on whom ye depend for safety, behold ye know that I have spoken unto you exceeding many things. —*II. Nephi vi: 2.*

Called by prophesy and by revelation.

And it came to pass that there was a man among them whose name was Abinadi; and he went forth among them, and began to prophesy, saying, Behold, thus saith the Lord, and thus hath he commanded me, saying, Go forth and say unto this people, thus saith the Lord: Wo be unto this people, for I have seen their abominations, and their wickedness, and their whoredoms; and except they repent, I will visit them in mine anger.—*Mosiah xi: 20.*

Now it came to pass that after the sons of Mosiah had done all these things, they took a small number with them, and returned to their father, the king, and desired of him that he would grant unto them, that they might, with those whom

they had selected, go up to the land of
Nephi, that they might preach the things
which they had heard, and that they
might impart the word of God to their
brethren, the Lamanites.

And king Mosiah went and inquired
of the Lord, if he would let his sons go
up among the Lamanites to preach the
word.

Called by
prophesy
and by
revelation.

And the Lord said unto Mosiah, Let
them go up, for many shall believe on
their words, and they shall have eternal
life; and I will deliver thy sons out of
the hands of the Lamanites.—*Mosiah
xxviii: 1, 6-7.*

But this is not all; they had given
themselves to much prayer and fasting,
therefore they had the Spirit of prophecy,
and the Spirit of revelation, and when
they taught, they taught with power and
authority of God.—*Alma xviii: 3.*

Yea, and there was continual peace
among them, and exceeding great prosperity in the church because of their
heed and diligence which they gave unto
the word of God, which was declared
unto them by Helaman, and Shiblon,
and Corianton, and Ammon and his
brethren, &c.: yea, and by all those who
had been ordained by the holy order of
God, being baptized unto repentance,
and sent forth to preach among the
people, &c.—*Alma xlix: 30.*

Men called
and ordained
to preach
the Gospel,

And again the Lord called others, and
said unto them likewise; and he gave
unto them power to baptize. And he

And to
baptize,

said unto them, On this wise shall ye
baptize; and there shall be no disputations among you.

And to baptize, Verily I say unto you, that whoso repenteth of his sins through your words,
and desireth to be baptized in my name,
on this wise shall ye baptize them: behold ye shall go down and stand in the
water, and in my name shall ye baptize
them.

And now behold, these are the words
which ye shall say, calling them by name,
saying,

Having authority given me of Jesus
Christ, I baptize you in the name of the
Father, and of the Son, and of the Holy
Ghost. Amen.

And then shall ye immerse them in
the water, and come forth again out of
the water.—*III. Nephi xi: 22-26.*

And now it came to pass that Alma
took Helam, he being one of the first,
and went and stood forth in the water,
and cried, saying, O Lord, pour out thy
Spirit upon thy servant, that he may do
this work with holiness of heart.

And when he had said these words,
the Spirit of the Lord was upon him,
and he said, Helam, I baptize thee,
having authority from the Almighty God,
as a testimony that ye have entered into
a covenant to serve him until you are
dead, as to the mortal body; and may
the Spirit of the Lord be poured out
upon you; and may he grant unto you
eternal life, through the redemption of

Christ, whom he has prepared from the foundation of the world.—*Mosiah xviii: 12-13.*

And it came to pass that when Jesus had made an end of these sayings, he touched with his hand the disciples whom he had chosen, one by one, even until he had touched them all, and spake unto them as he touched them;

And to confer the Holy Ghost.

And the multitude heard not the words which he spake, therefore they did not bear record; but the disciples bear record that he gave them power to give the Holy Ghost. And I will shew unto you hereafter that this record is true.—*III. Nephi xviii: 36-37.*

The words of Christ, which he spake unto his disciples, the twelve whom he had chosen, as he laid his hands upon them.

And he called them by name, saying, Ye shall call on the Father, in my name, in mighty prayer; and after ye have done this, ye shall have power that on him whom ye shall lay your hands, ye shall give the Holy Ghost; and in my name shall ye give it, for thus do mine apostles.

Now Christ spake these words unto them at the time of his first appearing; and the multitude heard it not, but the disciples heard it; and on as many as they laid their hands, fell the Holy Ghost.—*Moroni ii: 1-3.*

The manner which the disciples, who were called the Elders of the church, ordained Priests and Teachers.

How authority was conferred.

After they had prayed unto the Father

in the name of Christ, they laid their hands upon them, and said,

In the name of Jesus Christ I ordain you to be a Priest; (or, if he be a Teacher,) I ordain you to be a Teacher, to preach repentance and remission of sins through Jesus Christ, by the endurance of faith on his name to the end.

And after this manner did they ordain Priests and Teachers, according to the gifts and callings of God unto men; and they ordained them by the power of the Holy Ghost, which was in them.—*Moroni iii: 1-4.*

How author-
ity was
conferred.
And now it came to pass that after Alma had made an end of speaking unto the people of the church, which was established in the city of Zarahemla, he ordained Priests and Elders, by laying on his hands according to the order of God, to preside and watch over the church.—*Alma vi: 1.*

Wherefore I, Jacob, gave unto them these words as I taught them in the temple, having firstly obtained mine errand from the Lord.

For I, Jacob, and my brother Joseph, had been consecrated Priests and Teachers of this people, by the hand of Nephi.—*Jacob i: 17-18.*

CHURCH ORGANIZATION.

And it came to pass that as the disciples of Jesus were journeying and
were preaching the things which they
had both heard and seen, and were baptizing in the name of Jesus, it came to
pass that the disciples were gathered
together, and were united in mighty
prayer and fasting.

Name of the
Church—the
Church of
Jesus Christ.

And Jesus again shewed himself unto
them, for they were praying unto the
Father in his name; and Jesus came and
stood in the midst of them, and said
unto them, What will ye that I shall
give unto you?

And they said unto him, Lord we will
that thou wouldst tell us the name
whereby we shall call this church; for
there are disputations among the people
concerning this matter.

And the Lord said unto them, Verily,
verily I say unto you, why is it that the
people should murmur and dispute because of this thing?

Therefore whatsoever ye shall do, ye
shall do it in my name; therefore ye
shall call the church in my name; and
ye shall call upon the Father in my name.
that he will bless the church for my sake;

And how be it my church, save it be
called in my name? for if a church be
called in Moses' name, then it be Moses'
church; or if it be called in the name of

a man, then it be the church of a man; but if it be called in my name, then it is my church, if it so be that they are built upon my gospel.—*III. Nephi xxvii 1-4, 7-8.*

Officers of the Church:

And I saw the heavens open, and the Lamb of God descending out of heaven; and he came down and shewed himself unto them.

Twelve Apostles.

And I also saw and bear record, that the Holy Ghost fell upon twelve others; and they were ordained of God, and chosen.—*I. Nephi xii: 6-7.*

And it came to pass that when Jesus had spoken these words unto Nephi, and to those who had been called, (now the number of them who had been called, and received power and authority to baptize, were twelve,) and behold he stretched forth his hand unto the multitude, and cried unto them, saying, Blessed are ye if ye shall give heed unto the words of these twelve whom I have chosen from among you to minister unto you, and to be your servants; and unto them I have given power, that they may baptize you with water; and after that ye are baptized with water, behold I will baptize you with fire and with the Holy Ghost; therefore blessed are ye if ye shall believe in me, and be baptized, after that ye have seen me and know that I am.—*III. Nephi xii: 1.*

And it came to pass that on the morrow, when the multitude was gathered together, behold, Nephi and his brother whom he had raised from the dead, whose name was Timothy, and also his son, whose name was Jonas, and also Mathoni, and Mathonihah, his brother, and Kumeu, and Kumenonhi, and Jeremiah, and Shemnon, and Jonas, and Zedekiah, and Isaiah; now these were the names of the disciples whom Jesus had chosen. And it came to pass that they went forth and stood in the midst of the multitude.—*III. Nephi xix: 4.* *Names of the Twelve.*

And there were exceeding many prophets among us. And the people were a stiffnecked people, hard to understand.—*Enos i: 22.* *Prophets, Seers and Revelators.*

Now it was the custom among all the Nephites, to appoint for their chief captains, save it were in their times of wickedness, some one that had the Spirit of revelation, and also prophecy; therefore this Gidgiddoni was a great prophet among them, and also was the Chief Judge.—*III. Nephi iii: 19.*

Now Ammon said unto him, I can assuredly tell thee, O king, of a man that can translate the records; for he has wherewith that he can look, and translate all records that are of ancient date; and it is a gift from God. And the things are called interpreters, and no man can look in them, except he be commanded, lest he should look for that he ought not, and he should perish. And whosoever is commanded to look in them, the same is called seer.

Prophets, Seers and Revelators.

And behold, the king of the people who is in the land of Zarahemla, is the man that is commanded to do these things and who has this high gift from God.

And the king said, that a seer is greater than a prophet.

And Ammon said, that a seer is a revelator and a prophet also; and a gift which is greater can no man have, except he should possess the power of God, which no man can; yet a man may have great power given him from God.

But a seer can know of things which have past, and also of things which are to come, and by them shall all things be revealed, or, rather, shall secret things be made manifest, and hidden things shall come to light, and things which are not known shall be made known by them, and also things shall be made known by them which otherwise could not be known.—*Mosiah viii: 13-17.*

High Priests

And it came to pass that they were brought before the Priests, and delivered up unto the Priests by the Teachers; and the Priests brought them before Alma, who was the High Priest.—*Mosiah xxvi: 7.*

Now as I said concerning the holy order of this High Priesthood: there were many who were ordained and became High Priests of God; and it was on account of their exceeding faith and repentance, and their righteousness before God, they choosing to repent and work righteousness, rather than to perish.—*Alma xiii: 10.*

Now this was the cause of much afflic-   Elders.
tion to Alma, yea, and to many of the people whom Alma had consecrated to be Teachers, and Priests, and Elders over the church; yea, many of them were sorely grieved for the wickedness which they saw had begun to be among their people.

And he selected a wise man who was among the Elders of the church, and gave him power according to the voice of the people, that he might have power to enact laws, according to the laws which had been given, and to put them in force, according to the wickedness and the crimes of the people.—*Alma iv: 7, 16.*

And now I speak concerning baptism. Behold, Elders, Priests, and Teachers were baptized; and they were not baptized, save they brought forth fruit meet that they were worthy of it.

And they were strict to observe that there should be no iniquity among them; and whoso was found to commit iniquity, and three witnesses of the church did condemn them before the Elders; and if they repented not, and confessed not their names were blotted out, and they were not numbered among the people of Christ.—*Moroni vi: 1, 7.*

Priests.

And it came to pass that I, Nephi, did consecrate Jacob and Joseph, that they should be Priests and Teachers over the land of my people.—*II. Nephi v: 26.*

And again: It came to pass that when king Benjamin had made an end of all these things, and had consecrated his son Mosiah, to be a ruler and a king over his people, and had given him all the charges, concerning the kingdom, and also had appointed Priests to teach the people, that thereby they might hear and know the commandments of God, and to stir them up in remembrance of the oath which they had made, he dismissed the multitude, and they returned, every one, according to their families, to their own houses.—*Mosiah vi: 3.*

Teachers.

The manner which the disciples, who were called the Elders of the church, ordained Priests and Teachers.

After they had prayed unto the Father in the name of Christ, they laid their hands upon them, and said,

In the name of Jesus Christ I ordain you to be a Priest; (or, if he be a Teacher,) I ordain you to be a Teacher, to preach repentance and remission of sins through Jesus Christ, by the endurance of faith on his name to the end.

And after this manner did they ordain Priests and Teachers, according to the gifts and callings of God unto men; and they ordained them by the power of the Holy Ghost, which was in them.—*Moroni iii: 1-4.*

APOSTASY FROM THE GOSPEL.

And I also beheld a straight and narrow path, which came along by the rod
of iron, even to the tree by which I
stood; and it also led by the head of the
fountain, unto a large and spacious
field, as if it had been a world;

And I saw numberless concourses of
people: many of whom were pressing
forward, that they might obtain the path
which led unto the tree by which I
stood.

And it came to pass that they did
come forth, and commence in the path
which led to the tree.

And it came to pass that there arose a
mist of darkness; yea, even an exceeding great mist of darkness, insomuch
that they who had commenced in the
path, did lose their way, that they
wandered off and were lost.—*I. Nephi
viii: 20-23.*

Lehi's vision
of the
apostasy.

And while the angel spake these
words, I beheld and saw that the seed
of my brethren did contend against my
seed, according to the word of the angel;
and because of the pride of my seed,
and the temptations of the devil, I beheld that the seed of my brethren did
overpower the people of my seed.

And it came to pass that I beheld and
saw the people of the seed of my
brethren, that they had overcome my

Nephi's
vision of the
apostasy.

seed; and they went forth in multitudes upon the face of the land.

And I saw them gathered together in multitudes; and I saw wars and rumors of wars among them; and in wars and rumors of wars, I saw many generations pass away.

And the angel said unto me, Behold these shall dwindle in unbelief.

And it came to pass that I beheld after they had dwindled in unbelief, they became a dark, and loathsome, and a filthy people, full of idleness and all manner of abominations.—*I. Nephi xii:* *19-23.*

Universal apostasy foretold.

But, behold, in the last days, or in the days of the Gentiles; yea, behold all the nations of the Gentiles, and also the Jews, both those who shall come upon this land, and those who shall be upon other lands; yea, even upon all the lands of the. earth; behold, they will be drunken with iniquity, and all manner of abominations.*—*II. Nephi xxvii: I.*

Then Alma said unto him, Blessed art thou; and the Lord shall prosper thee in this land.

But behold, I have somewhat to prophesy unto thee; but what I prophesy

---

* The Church of England states in one of her homilies, "that laity and clergy, learned and unlearned, men and women, and children of all ages, sects and degrees, of WHOLE CHRISTENDOM, have been at once buried in the MOST ABOMINABLE IDOLATRY (a most dreadful thing to think), and that for the SPACE OF EIGHT HUNDRED YEARS OR MORE."—*Homily on the Perils of Idolatry.*

unto thee, ye shall not make known; yea, what I prophesy unto thee shall not be made known, even until the prophecy is fulfilled; therefore write the words which I shall say.

And these are the words: Behold, I perceive that this very people, the Nephites, according to the Spirit of revelation which is in me, in four hundred years from the time that Jesus Christ shall manifest himself unto them, shall dwindle in unbelief;

Yea, and then shall they see wars and pestilences, yea, famines and bloodshed, even until the people of Nephi shall become extinct;

Yea, and this because they shall dwindle in unbelief, and fall into the works of darkness. and lasciviousness, and all manner of iniquities; yea, I say unto you, that because they shall sin against so great light and knowledge; yea, I say unto you, that from that day, even the fourth generation shall not all pass away, before this great iniquity shall come;

And when that great day cometh, behold, the time very soon cometh that those who are now, or the seed of those who are now numbered among the people of Nephi, shall no more be numbered among the people of Nephi;

But whosoever remaineth, and is not destroyed in that great and dreadful day, shall be numbered among the Lamanites, and shall become like unto them, all, save it be a few, who shall be called the

Universal apostasy foretold.

disciples of the Lord; and them shall the Lamanites pursue, even until they shall become extinct. And now, because of iniquity, this prophecy shall be fulfilled. —*Alma xlv: 8-14.*

Beginning of the apostasy.
And when my father saw that the waters of the river emptied into the fountain of the Red Sea, he spake unto Laman, saying, O that thou mightest be like unto this river, continually running into the fountain of all righteousness.

And he also spake unto Lemuel: O that thou mightest be like unto this valley, firm and steadfast, and immoveable in keeping the commandments of the Lord.

Now this he spake because of the stiffneckedness of Laman and Lemuel; for behold they did murmur in many things against their father, because he was a visionary man, and had led them out of the land of Jerusalem, to leave the land of their inheritance, and their gold, and their silver, and their precious things, to perish in the wilderness. And this they said he had done because of the foolish imaginations of his heart.

And thus Laman and Lemuel, being the eldest, did murmur against their father. And they did murmur because they knew not the dealings of that God who had created them.—*I. Nephi ii: 9-12.*

Behold, it came to pass that I, Nephi, did cry much unto the Lord my God, because of the anger of my brethren.

But behold, their anger did increase

against me; insomuch that they did seek to take away my life.

And it came to pass that the Lord did warn me, that I, Nephi, should depart from them, and flee into the wilderness, and all those who would go with me.— II. *Nephi v: 1-2, 5.*

And now it came to pass that the people of Nephi, under the reign of the second king, began to grow hard in their hearts, and indulge themselves somewhat in wicked practices, such as like unto David of old, desiring many wives and concubines, and also Solomon, his son:

Yea, and they also began to search much gold and silver, and began to be lifted up somewhat in pride.—*Jacob i: 15-16.*

Apostasy increasing.

Now the sons of Mosiah were numbered among the unbelievers; and also one of the sons of Alma was numbered among them, he being called Alma, after his father; nevertheless, he became a very wicked and an idolatrous man. And he was a man of many words, and did speak much flattery to the people; therefore he led many of the people to do after the manner of his iniquities.

And he became a great hinderment to the prosperity of the church of God; stealing away the hearts of the people; causing much dissension among the people; giving a chance for the enemy of God to exercise his power over them.— *Mosiah xxvii: 8-9.*

Apostasy spreading.

Apostasy
spreading.

And now it came to pass that after Helaman and his brethren had appointed priests and teachers over the churches that there arose a dissension among them, and they would not give heed to the words of Helaman and his brethren;

But they grew proud, being lifted up in their hearts, because of their exceeding great riches; therefore they grew rich in their own eyes, and would not give heed to their words, to walk uprightly before God.—*Alma xlv: 23-24.*

Prophets
cast out.

Yea, wo unto this people, because of this time which has arrived, that ye do cast out the prophets, and do mock them, and cast stones at them, and do slay them, and do all manner of iniquity unto them, even as they did of old time.

And now when ye talk, ye say, If our days had been in the days of our fathers of old, ye would not have slain the prophets; ye would not have stoned them and cast them out.

Behold ye are worse than they; for as the Lord liveth, if a prophet come among you, and declareth unto you the word of the Lord, which testifieth of your sins and iniquities, ye are angry with him, and cast him out, and seek all manner of ways to destroy him; yea, you will say that he is a false prophet, and that he is a sinner, and of the devil, because he testifieth that your deeds are evil.—*Helaman xiii: 24-26.*

And it came to pass that the brother of Shiblom caused that all the prophets who prophesied of the destruction of the people, should be put to death.— *Ether xi: 5.*

And it came to pass in the fifty and fourth year there were many dissensions in the church, and there was also a contention among the people, insomuch that there was much bloodshed;

Now this great loss of the Nephites, and the great slaughter which was among them, would not have happened, had it not been for their wickedness, and their abomination which was among them; yea, and it was among those also who professed to belong to the church of God;

And it was because of the pride of their hearts, because of their exceeding riches, yea, it was because of their oppression to the poor, withholding' their food from the hungry, withholding their clothing from the naked, and smiting their humble brethren upon the cheek, making a mock of that which was sacred, denying the Spirit of prophecy and of revelation, murdering, plundering, lying, stealing, committing adultery, rising up in great contentions, and deserting away into the land of Nephi, among the Lamanites;

And because of this their great wickedness, and their boastings in their own strength, they were left in their own strength; therefore they did not prosper, but were afflicted and smitten, and driven before the Lamanites, until they had lost possession of almost all their lands.

Sessation of spiritual gifts. And that they had altered and trampled under their feet the laws of Mosiah, or that which the Lord commanded him to give unto the people; and thus seeing that their laws had become corrupted, and that they had become a wicked people, insomuch that they were wicked even like unto the Lamanites.

And because of their iniquity, the church had begun to dwindle; and they began to disbelieve in the Spirit of prophecy, and in the Spirit of revelation; and the judgments of God did stare them in the face.

And they saw that they had become weak, like unto their brethren, the Lamanites, and that the Spirit of the Lord did no more preserve them; yea, it had withdrawn from them because the Spirit of the Lord doth not dwell in unholy temples. —*Helaman iv: I, 11-13, 22-24.*

Church broken up. And thus there became a great inequality in all the land, insomuch that the church began to be broken up; yea, insomuch that in the thirtieth year the church was broken up in all the land, save it were among a few of the Lamanites, who were converted unto the true faith; and they would not depart from it, for they were firm and steadfast, and immoveable, willing with all diligence

to keep the commandments of the
Lord.

Now the cause of this iniquity of the
people, was this, Satan had great power,
unto the stirring up of the people to do
all manner of iniquity, and to the puffing
them up with pride, tempting them to
seek for power, and authority, and riches,
and the vain things of the world.—*III.
Nephi vi: 14-15.*

And it came to pass that when two
hundred and ten years had passed away
there were many churches in the land;
yea, there were many churches which
professed to know the Christ, and yet
they did deny the more parts of his
Gospel, insomuch that they did receive
all manner of wickedness, and did administer that which was sacred unto him
to whom it had been forbidden because
of unworthiness.—*IV. Nephi i: 27.*

Nephites deny the gospel.

And now, after that they have all
dwindled in unbelief, and there is none,
save it be the Lamanites, and they have
rejected the Gospel of Christ; therefore
1 am commanded that I should hide
them up again in the earth.—*Ether iv: 3.*

Apostasy universal.

And there are none that do know the
true God, save it be the disciples of
Jesus, who did tarry in the land until
the wickedness of the people was so
great, that the Lord would not suffer
them to remain with the people; and
whether they be upon the face of the
land no man knoweth.—*Mormon viii: 10.*

RESTORATION OF THE GOSPEL.

Prophecies foretelling the restoration of the gospel.

Neither will the Lord God suffer that the Gentiles shall for ever remain in that awful state of blindness, which thou beholdest they are in, because of the plain and most precious parts of the gospel of the Lamb which have been kept back by that abominable church, whose formation thou hast seen.

And it came to pass that the angel of the Lord spake unto me, saying, Behold, saith the Lamb of God, after I have visited the remnant of the house of Israel, and this remnant of whom 1 speak, is the seed of thy father; wherefore, after I have visited them in judgment, and smitten them by the hand of the Gentiles; and after the Gentiles do stumble exceedingly, because of the most plain and precious parts of the gospel of the Lamb, which have been kept back by that abominable church, which is the mother of harlots, saith the Lamb; I will be merciful unto the Gentiles in that day, insomuch that I will bring forth unto them in mine own power,.much of my gospel, which shall be plain and precious, saith the Lamb;

For behold, saith the Lamb, I will manifest myself unto thy seed, that they shall write many things which I shall minister unto them, which shall be plain and precious; and after thy seed shall be destroyed, and dwindle in unbelief, and also the seed of thy brethren; behold, these things shall be hid up, to come forth unto the Gentiles, by the gift and power of the Lamb;

And in them shall be written my gospel, saith the Lamb, and my rock and my salvation.—*I. Nephi xiii: 32, 34-36.*

And the Lord will set his hand again the second time to restore his people from their lost and fallen state. Wherefore he will proceed to do a marvelous work and a wonder among the children of men.

Wherefore, he shall bring forth his words unto them, which words shall judge them at the last day, for they shall be given them for the purpose of convincing them of the true Messiah, who was rejected by them; and unto the convincing of them that they need not look forward any more for a Messiah to come, for there should not any come, save it should be a false Messiah, which should deceive the people: for there is save one Messiah spoken of by the prophets, and that Messiah is he who should be rejected by the Jews.—*II. Nephi xxv: 17-18.*

But behold, I prophesy unto you concerning the last days; concerning the days when the Lord God shall bring these things forth unto the children of men.

After my seed and the seed of my

Prophecies foretelling the restoration of the gospel.

When to be restored.

brethren shall have dwindled in unbelief, and shall have been smitten by the Gentiles; yea, after the Lord God shall have camped against them round about, and shall have laid siege against them with a mount, and raised forts against them; and after they shall have been brought down low in the dust, even that they are not, yet the words of the righteous shall be written, and the prayers of the faithful shall be heard, and all those who have dwindled in unbelief, shall not be forgotten;

For those who shall be destroyed shall speak unto them out of the ground, and their speech shall be low out of the dust, and their voice shall be as one that hath a familiar spirit; for the Lord God will give unto him power, that he may whisper concerning them, even as it were out of the ground; and their speech shall whisper out of the dust.—II. *Nephi xxvi: 14-16.*

When to be restored.

And no one need say, They shall not come, for they surely shall, for the Lord hath spoken it; for out of the earth shall they come, by the hand of the Lord, and none can stay it; and it shall come in a day when it shall be said that miracles are done away; and it shall come even as if one should speak from the dead.—*Mormon viii: 26.*

To whom restored.

And now, I, Nephi, speak concerning the prophecies of which my father hath spoken, concerning Joseph, who was carried into Egypt.—*II. Nephi iv: 1.*

For Joseph truly testified, saying: A seer shall the Lord my God raise up, who shall be a choice seer unto the fruit of my loins.

To whom restored.

Yea, Joseph truly said, Thus saith the Lord unto me: A choice seer will I raise up out of the fruit of thy loins; and he shall be esteemed highly among the fruit of thy loins. And unto him will I give commandment, that he shall do a work for the fruit of thy loins, his brethren, which shall be of great worth unto them, even to the bringing of them to the knowledge of the covenants which I have made with thy fathers.

And thus prophesied Joseph, saying: Behold, that seer will the Lord bless; and they that seek to destroy him, shall be confounded; for this promise, which I have obtained of the Lord, of the fruit of my loins, shall be fulfilled. Behold, I am sure of the fulfilling of this promise.

And his name shall be called after me: and it shall be after the name of his father. And he shall be like unto me; for the thing which the Lord shall bring forth by his hand, by the power of the Lord shall bring my people unto salvation.—*Il. Nephi iii: 6-7, 14-15.*

And it shall come to pass that the Lord God shall bring forth unto you the words of a book, and they shall be the words of them which have slumbered.

A book to come forth

And behold the book shall be sealed: and in the book shall be a revelation from God, from the beginning of the world to the ending thereof.

Wherefore, because of the things which are sealed up, the things which are sealed shall not be delivered in the day of the wickedness and abominations of the people. Wherefore the book shall be kept from them.

But the book shall be delivered unto a man, and he shall deliver the words of the book, which are the words of those who have slumbered in the dust; and he shall deliver these words unto another.— II. *Nephi xxvii: 6-9.*

Out of the Earth

For those who shall be destroyed shall speak unto them out of the ground, and their speech shall be low out of the dust, and their voice shall be as one that hath a familiar spirit; for the Lord God will give unto him power, that he may whisper concerning them, even as it were out of the ground; and their speech shall whisper out of the dust.—II. *Nephi xxvi: 16.*

And no one need say, They shall not come, for they surely shall, for the Lord hath spoken it; for out of the earth shall they come, by the hand of the Lord, and none can stay it; and it shall come in a day when it shall be said that miracles are done away; and it shall come even as if one should speak from the dead.—*Mormon viii: 26.*

Three witnesses to behold the book.

Wherefore, at that day when the book shall be delivered unto the man of whom I have spoken, the book shall be hid from the eyes of the world, that the eyes of none shall behold it save it be that three witnesses* shall behold it, by the power of God, besides him to whom the book shall be delivered; and they shall testify to the truth of the book and the things therein.—II. *Nephi xxvii: 12.*

And behold, ye may be privileged that ye may show the plates unto those who shall assist to bring forth this work;

And unto three shall they be shewn by the power of God; wherefore they shall

---

*THE TESTIMONY OF THREE WITNESSES:—Be it known unto all nations, kindreds, tongues, and people unto whom this work shall come, that we, through the grace of God, the Father, and our Lord Jesus Christ, have seen the plates which contain this record, which is a record of the people of Nephi, and also of the Lamanites, their brethren, and also of the people of Jared, who came from the tower of which hath been spoken; and we also know that they have been translated by the gift and power of God, for his voice hath declared it unto us, wherefore we know of a surety that the work is true. And we also testify that we have seen the engravings which are upon the plates; and they have been shewn unto us by the power of God, and not of man. And we declare with words of soberness, that an angel of God came down from heaven, and he brought and laid before our eyes, that we beheld and saw the plates, and the engravings thereon; and we know that it is by the grace of God the Father, and our Lord Jesus Christ, that we beheld and bear record that these things are true, and it is marvelous in our eyes, nevertheless the voice of the Lord commanded us that we should bear record of it, wherefore, to be obedient unto the commandments of God, we bear testimony of these things. And we know that if we are faithful in Christ, we shall rid our garments of the blood of all men, and be found spotless before the judgment seat of Christ, and shall dwell with him eternally in the heavens. And the honor be to the Father, and to the Son, and to the Holy Ghost, which is one God. Amen.

OLIVER COWDERY,
DAVID WHITMER,
MARTIN HARRIS.

know of a surety that these things are true.

And in the mouth of three witnesses shall these things be established; and the testimony of three, and this work, in the which shall be shewn forth the power of God, and also his word, of which the Father, and the Son, and the Holy Ghost beareth record; and all this shall stand as a testimony against the world at the last day.—*Ether v: 2-4.*

Other witnesses.

And there is none other which shall view it, save it be a few* according to the will of God, to bear testimony of his word unto the children of men: for the Lord God hath said, That the words of the faithful should speak as if it were from the dead.

Wherefore, the Lord God will proceed to bring forth the words of the book;

---

* THE TESTIMONY OF EIGHT WITNESSES:—Be it known unto all nations, kindreds, tongues, and people unto whom this work shall come, that Joseph Smith, Jun., the translator of this work, has shewn unto us the plates of which hath been spoken, which have the appearance of gold, and as many of the leaves as the said Smith has translated, we did handle with our hands; and we also saw the engravings thereon, all of which has the appearance of ancient work, and of curious workmanship. And this we bear record with words of soberness, that the said Smith has shewn unto us, for we have seen and hefted, and know of a surety that the said Smith has got the plates of which we have spoken. And we give our names unto the world, to witness unto the world that which we have seen; and we lie not, God bearing witness of it.

CHRISTIAN WHITMER,   HIRAM PAGE,
JACOB WHITMER,   JOSEPH SMITH, Sen.
PETER WHITMER, Jun.,   HYRUM SMITH,
JOHN WHITMER,   SAMUEL H. SMITH.

and in the mouth of as many witnesses
as seemeth him good, will he establish
his word; and wo be unto him that re-
jecteth the word of God.—*II. Nephi
xxvii*: 13-14.

Wherefore it is an abridgment of the
record of the people of Nephi, and also
of the Lamanites; written to the Lamanites who are a remnant of the house of
Israel; and also to Jew and Gentile:
written by way of commandment, and
also by the Spirit of prophecy and of
revelation. Written and sealed up, and
hid up unto the Lord, that they might
not be destroyed; to come forth by the
gift and power of God unto the interpretation thereof: sealed by the hand of
Moroni, and hid up unto the Lord, to
come forth in due time by the way of
Gentile; the interpretation thereof by
the gift of God.

What the
book is.

An abridgment taken from the Book
of Ether also; which is a record of the
people of Jared; who were scattered at
the time the Lord confounded the
language of the people when they were
building a tower to get to heaven; which
is to shew unto the remnant of the
House of Israel what great things the
Lord hath done for their fathers; and
that they may know the covenants of
the Lord, that they are not cast off for-
ever; and also to the convincing of the
Jew and Gentile that Jesus is the Christ,
the Eternal God, manifesting himself
unto all nations. And now if there are

faults, they are the mistakes of men: wherefore condemn not the things of God, that ye may be found spotless at the judgment-seat of Christ.—*Book of Mormon, title page.*

Object of the book—to establish the truth of the Bible,

And it came to pass that I beheld the remnant of the seed of my brethren, and also the book of the Lamb of God, which had proceeded forth from the mouth of the Jew, that it came forth from the Gentiles, unto the remnant of the seed of my brethren,

And after it had come forth unto them, I beheld other books, which came forth by the power of the Lamb, from the Gentiles unto them, unto the convincing of the Gentiles, and the remnant of the seed of my brethren, and also the Jews, who were scattered upon all the face of the earth, that the records of the prophets and of the twelve apostles of the Lamb are true.

And the angel spake unto me, saying, These last records which thou hast seen among the Gentiles, shall establish the truth of the first, which are of the twelve apostles of the Lamb, and shall make known the plain and precious things which have been taken away from them; and shall make known to all kindreds, tongues, and people, that the Lamb of God is the Son of the Eternal Father, and the Savior of the world; and that all men must come unto him, or they cannot be saved.—*I. Nephi xiii: 38-40.*

But a seer will I raise up out of the

fruit of thy loins; and unto him will I give power to bring forth my word unto the seed of thy loins; and not to the bringing forth my word only, saith the Lord, but to the convincing them of my word, which shall have already gone forth among them.

Wherefore, the fruit of thy loins shall write; and the fruit of the loins of Judah shall write; and that which shall be written by the fruit of thy loins, and also that which shall be written by the fruit of the loins of Judah, shall grow together, unto the confounding of false doctrines, and laying down of contentions, and establishing peace among the fruit of thy loins, and bringing them to the knowledge of their fathers in the latter days; and also to the knowledge of my covenants, saith the Lord.

And his name shall be called after me: and it shall be after the name of his father. And he shall be like unto me; for the thing which the Lord shall bring forth by the power of the Lord shall bring my people unto salvation;

Yea, thus prophesied Joseph, I am sure of this thing, even as I am sure of the promise of Moses; for the Lord hath said unto me, I will preserve thy seed for ever.—II. *Nephi iii: 11-12, 15-16.*

Confound false doctrines, establish peace, and bring people unto salvation.

THE SCATTERING OF ISRAEL.

Predictions concerning the gathering of Israel.

Yea, even my father spake much concerning the Gentiles, and also concerning the house of Israel, that they should be compared like unto an olive tree, whose branches should be broken off, and should be scattered upon all the face of the earth.

Wherefore, he said it must needs be that we should be led with one accord into the land of promise unto the fulfilling of the word of the Lord, that we should be scattered upon all the face of the earth.—*I. Nephi x: 12-13.*

For behold, thus saith the Lord, I will liken thee, O house of Israel, like unto a tame olive tree, which a man took and nourished in his vineyard; and it grew, and waxed old, and began to decay.

And it came to pass that the master of the vineyard went forth, and he saw that his olive tree began to decay; and he said, I will prune it, and dig about it, and nourish it, that perhaps it may shoot forth young and tender branches, and it perish not.

And it came to pass that he pruned it, and digged about it, and nourished it according to his word.

And it came to pass that after many days, it began to put forth somewhat a little, young and tender branches; but behold, the main top thereof began to perish.

And behold, saith the Lord of the vineyard, I take away many of these young and tender branches, and. I will graft them whithersoever I will;* and it mattereth not that if it so be, that the root of this tree will perish, I may preserve the fruit thereof unto myself; wherefore, I will take these young and tender branches, and I will graft them whithersoever I will.

And these will I place in the nethermost part of my vineyard, whithersoever I will, it mattereth not unto thee; and I do it that I might preserve unto myself the natural branches of the tree; and also, that I may lay up fruit thereof, against the season, unto myself: for it grieveth me that I should lose this tree and the fruit thereof.

And it came to pass that the Lord of the vineyard went his way, and hid the natural branches† of the tame olive tree in the nethermost parts of the vineyard; some in one, and some in another, according to his will and pleasure.

And it came to pass that the servant said unto his master, How comest thou hither to plant this tree, or this branch

---

* Upon isles distant from Palestine.

† Ten tribes in the North. Some of Judah and Joseph in America. Others, upon isles.

cf the tree? for behold, it was the poor-
est spot* in all the land of the vineyard.

And the Lord of the vineyard said
unto him, Counsel me not: I knew
that it was a poor spot of ground;
wherefore, I said unto thee, I have
nourished it this long time, and thou
beholdest that it hath brought forth forth
much fruit.

And it came to pass that the Lord of
the vineyard said unto his servant, Look
hither; behold I have planted another
branch of the tree also; and thou knowest that this spot † of ground was poorer
than the first. But, behold the tree: I
have nourished it this long time, and it
hath brought forth much fruit; therefore, gather it, and lay it up, against the
season, that I may preserve it unto mine
own self.

And it came to pass that the Lord of
the vineyard said again unto his servant,
Look hither, and behold another branch ‡
also, which I have planted; behold
that, I have nourished it also, and it
hath brought forth fruit.—*Jacob v: 3-6,
8, 13-14, 21-24.*

Wherefore, the things of which I have
read, are things pertaining to things
both temporal and spiritual; for it
appears that the house of Israel, sooner

* Place unknown.
† Place unknown.
‡ Place unknown.

or later, will be scattered upon all the face of the earth, and also among all nations.

And behold there are many who are already lost from the knowledge of those who are at Jerusalem. Yea, the more part of all the tribes have been led away; and they are scattered to and fro upon the isles of the sea; and whither they are, none of us knoweth, save that we know that they have been led away.

Scattering of Israel.

And since they have been led away, these things have been prophesied concerning them, and also concerning all those who shall hereafter be scattered and be confounded, because of the Holy one of Israel; for against him will they harden their hearts; wherefore, they shall be scattered among all nations, and shall be hated of all men.

And it meaneth that the time cometh that after all the house of Israel have been scattered and confounded, that the Lord God will raise up a mighty nation among the Gentiles, yea, even upon the face of this land; and by them shall our seed be scattered.—*I. Nephi xxii: 3-5, 7.*

But behold, when the time cometh that they shall dwindle in unbelief, after they have received so great blessings from the hand of the Lord; having a knowledge of the creation of the earth, and all men, knowing the great and marvellous works of the Lord from the creation of the world; having power given them to do all things by faith; having all the commandments from the beginning, and having been brought by his infinite goodness into this precious land of promise; behold, I say, if the day shall come that they will reject the Holy One of Israel, the true Messiah, their Redeemer and their God, behold the judgments of him that is just shall rest upon them;

Scattering of Israel. Yea, he will bring other nations unto them, and he will give unto them power, and he will take away from them the lands of their possessions; and he will cause them to be scattered and smitten.— II. *Nephi i: 10-11.*

O repent ye, repent ye! why will ye die? Turn ye, turn ye unto the Lord your God.   Why has he forsaken you?

And behold instead of gathering you, except ye will repent, behold he shall scatter you forth that ye shall become meat for dogs and wild beasts.—*Helaman vii: 17, 19.*

And also that the seed of this people may more fully believe his gospel, which shall go forth unto them from the Gentiles; for this people shall be scattered, and shall become a dark, a filthy, and a loathsome people, beyond the description of that which ever hath been amongst us; yea, even that which hath been among the Lamanites; and this because of their unbelief and idolatry. —*Mormon v: 15.*

GATHERING OF ISRAEL.

Yea, even my father spake much concerning the Gentiles, and also concerning the house of Israel, that they should be compared like unto an olive tree, whose branches should be broken off, and should be scattered upon all the face of the earth.

And after the house of Israel should be scattered, they should be gathered together again; or, in fine, after the Gentiles had received the fulness of the Gospel, the natural branches of the olive tree, or the remnants of the house of Israel, should be grafted in, or come to the knowledge of the true Messiah, their Lord and their Redeemer.—*I. Nephi x: 12, 14.*

Nevertheless, when that day cometh, saith the prophet, that they no more turn aside their hearts against the Holy One of Israel, then will he remember the covenants which he made to their fathers;

Yea, then will he remember the isles of the sea; yea, and all the people who are of the house of Israel, will I gather in, saith the Lord, according to the words of the prophet Zenos, from the four quarters of the earth.—*I. Nephi xix: 15-16.*

Wherefore, the Lord God will proceed to make bare his arm, in the eyes of all

Prophesies foretelling the gathering of Israel.

the nations, in bringing about his covenants and his gospel, unto those who are
of the house of Israel.

Prophesies
foretelling
the gather-
ing of Israel.
Wherefore, he will bring them again
out of captivity, and they shall be
gathered together to the lands of their
inheritance; and they shall be brought
out of obscurity and out of darkness;
and they shall know that the Lord is their
Savior and their Redeemer, the Mighty
One of Israel.

And he gathereth his children from the
four quarters of the earth; and he num-
bereth his sheep, and they know him;
and there shall be one fold and one
shepherd; and he shall feed his sheep,
and in him they shall find pasture.—*I.
Nephi xxii: 11-12, 25.*

And now, the words which I shall
read, are they which Isaiah spake concerning all the house of Israel; wherefore, they may be likened unto you, for
ye are of the house of Israel. And there
are many things which have been spoken
by Isaiah, which may be likened unto you,
because ye are of the house of Israel.

And now, these are the words: Thus
saith the Lord God: Behold, I will lift
up mine hand to the Gentiles, and set up
my standard to the people; and they
shall bring thy sons in their arms, and
thy daughters shall be carried upon their
shoulders.

And kings shall be thy nursing fathers,
and their queens thy nursing mothers;
they shall bow down to thee with their

faces towards the earth, and lick up the dust of thy feet; and thou shalt know that I am the Lord; for they shall not be ashamed that wait for me—*II Nephi vi: 5-7*

Israel to gather, in the last days, in the top of the mountains.

The word that Isaiah, the son of Amos, saw, concerning Judah and Jerusalem.

And it shall come to pass in the last days, when the mountain of the Lord's house shall be established in the top of the mountains, and shall be exalted above the hills, and all nations shall flow unto it.

And many people shall go and say, Come ye, and let us go up to the mountain of the Lord, to the house of the God of Jacob; and he will teach us of his ways, and we will walk in his paths: for out of Zion shall go forth the law, and the word of the Lord from Jerusalem. — II. *Nephi xii: 1-3.*

Thus saith the Lord, in an acceptable time have I heard thee, O isles of the sea, and in a day of salvation have I helped thee; and I will preserve thee, and give thee my servant for a covenant of the people, to establish the earth, to cause to inherit the desolate heritages;

That thou mayest say to the prisoners, Go forth; to them that sit in darkness, Shew yourselves. They shall feed in the ways, and their pastures shall be in all high places.

And I will make all my mountains a way, and my highways shall be exalted.

And then, O house of Israel, behold, these shall come from far; and lo, these from the north and from the west; and these from the land of Sinim.

Lift up thine eyes round about and behold; all these gather themselves to_gether, and· they shall come to thee. And as I live, saith the Lord, thou shalt surely clothe thee with them all, as with an ornament, and bind them on even as a bride.

For thy waste and thy desolate places, and the land of thy destruction, shall even now be too narrow by reason of the inhabitants; and they that swallowed thee up shall be far away.—*I. Nephi xxi: 8.9, II-12, 18-19.*

The Jews to gather to Jerusalem.

And it shall come to pass that the Jews which are scattered, also shall begin to believe in Christ; and they shall begin to gather in upon the face of the land; and as many as shall believe in Christ, shall also become a delightsome people.—*II. Nephi xxx: 7.*

And now, my beloved brethren, I have read these things that ye might know concerning the covenants of the Lord; that he has covenanted with all the house of Israel;

That he has spoken unto the Jews, by the mouth of his holy prophets, even from the beginning down, from generation to generation, until the time comes that they shall be restored to the true church and fold of God; when they shall be gathered home to the lands of their inheritance, and shall be established in all their lands of promise.—*II. Nephi ix:. 1-2.*

But behold, thus saith the Lord God: When the day cometh that they shall believe in me, that I am Christ, then have I covenanted with their fathers that they shall be restored in the flesh, upon the earth, unto the lands of their inheritance.

And it shall come to pass that they shall be gathered in from their long dispersion, from the isles of the sea, and from the four parts of the earth; and the nations of the Gentiles shall be great in the eyes of me, saith God, in carrying them forth to the lands of their inheritance.

Yea, the kings of the Gentiles shall be nursing fathers unto them, and their queens shall become nursing mothers; wherefore, the promises of the Lord are great unto the Gentiles, for he hath spoken it, and who can dispute?—*II. Nephi x: 7-9.*

And I command you that ye shall write these sayings, after I am gone, that if it so be that my people at Jerusalem, they who have seen me, and been with me in my ministry, do not ask the Father in my name, that they may receive a knowledge of you by the Holy Ghost, and also of the other tribes whom they know not of, that these sayings which ye shall write, shall be kept, and shall be manifested unto the Gentiles, that through the fulness of the Gentiles, the remnant of their seed who shall be scattered forth upon the face of the earth,

The Jews to be gathered to Jerusalem

The Jews to be gathered to Jerusalem

because of their unbelief, may be brought in, or may be brought to a knowledge of me, their Redeemer.

And then will I gather them in from the four quarters of the earth; and then will I fulfil the covenant which the Father hath made unto all the people of the house of Israel.—*III. Nephi xvi: 4-5.*

And then shall the remnants which shall be scattered abroad upon the face of the earth, be gathered in from the east, and from the west, and from the south, and from the north; and they shall be brought to the knowledge of the Lord their God, who hath redeemed them.

And I will gather my people together, as a man gathereth his sheaves into the floor.

And I will remember the covenant which I have made with my people, and I have covenanted with them, that I would gather them together in mine own due time; that I would give unto them again the land of their fathers, for their inheritance, which is the land of Jerusalem, which is the promised land unto them for ever, saith the Father.

Verily, verily, I say unto you, all these things shall surely come, even as the Father hath commanded me. Then shall this covenant which the Father hath covenanted with his people, be fulfilled; and then shall Jerusalem be inhabited again with my people, and it shall be the land of their inheritance.— *III. Nephi xx: 13, 18, 29, 46.*

And verily, verily, I say unto you, that I have other sheep, which are not of this land; neither of the land of Jerusalem; neither in any parts of that land round about, whither I have been to minister.

For they of whom I speak, are they who have not as yet heard my voice; neither have I at any time manifested myself unto them.

But I have received a commandment of the Father, that I shall go unto them, and that they shall hear my voice, and shall be numbered among my sheep, that there may be one fold, and one shepherd; therefore I go to show myself unto them.—*III Nephi xvi: 1-3.*

But now I go unto the Father, and also to shew myself unto the lost tribes of Israel, for they are not lost unto the Father, for he knoweth whither he hath taken them.—*III. Nephi xvii: 4.*

And then shall the work of the Father commence at that day, even when this gospel shall be preached among the remnant of this people. Verily I say unto you, at that day shall the work of the Father commence among all the dispersed of my people; yea, even the tribes which have been lost, which the Father hath led away out of Jerusalem.

Yea, and then shall the work commence, with the Father, among all nations, in preparing the way whereby his people may be gathered home to the land of their inheritance.—III. *Nephi xxi: 26, 28.*

Restoration of the Lost Tribes.

And it shall come to pass that the
Jews shall have the words of the Nephites, and the Nephites shall have the
words of the Jews; and the Nephites
and the Jews shall have the words of the
lost tribes of Israel; and the lost tribes
of Israel shall have the words of the
Nephites and the Jews.

And it shall come to pass that my
people which are of the house of Israel,
shall be gathered home unto the lands
of their possessions; and my word also
shall be gathered in one. And I will
shew unto them that fight against my
word and against my people, who are of
the house of Israel, that I am God, and
that I covenanted with Abraham, that I
would remember his seed for ever.—*II.
Nephi xxix: 13-14.*

Behold, Ether saw the days of Christ,
and he spake concerning a New Jerusalem upon this land;

And that a New Jerusalem should be
built up upon this land, unto the remnant of the seed of Joseph; for which
things there has been a type.

And then also cometh the Jerusalem
of old; and the inhabitants thereof,
blessed are they, for they have been
washed in the blood of the Lamb; and
they are they who were scattered and
gathered in from the four quarters of the
earth, and from the north countries, and
are partakers of the fulfilling of the
covenant which God made with their
father Abraham.—*Ether xiii: 4, 6, 11.*

SECOND COMING OF CHRIST.

Behold, I will send you Elijah* the prophet before the coming of the great and dreadful day of the Lord; . Sign to precede Christ's second coming.

And he shall turn the heart of the fathers to the children, and the heart of the children to their fathers, lest I come and smite the earth with a curse.—III. *Nephi xxv: 5-6.*

And now it came to pass that when Jesus had told these things, he expounded them unto the multitude, and he did expound all things unto them, both great and small. Referred to by Jesus.

And he did expound all things, even from the beginning until the time that he should come in his glory; yea, even all things which should come upon the face of the earth, even until the elements should melt with fervent heat, and the earth should be wrapt together as a

---

* On April 6th, 1836, in the Kirtland Temple, Joseph Smith and Oliver Cowdery were given a number of heavenly visions, in one of which Elijah the prophet appeared. The following account of the vision is given by the Prophet Joseph: After this vision (vision of Elias) had closed, another great and glorious vision burst upon us, for Elijah the prophet, who was taken to heaven without tasting death, stood before us, and said, Behold, the time has fully come, which was spoken of by the mouth of Malachi, testifying that he (Elijah) should be sent before the great and dreadful day of the Lord come, to turn the hearts of the fathers to the children, and the children to the fathers, lest the whole earth be smitten with a curse. Therefore the keys of this dispensation are committed into your hands, and by this ye may know that the great and dreadful day of the Lord is near even at the doors.—*Doc, & Cov. cx: 13-16.*

scroll, and the heavens and the earth should pass away.—III. *Nephi xxvi: 1, 3.*

Second coming of Messiah.

And it shall come to pass that I will establish my people, O house of Israel.

And behold, this people will I establish in this land, unto the fulfilling of the covenant which I made with your father Jacob; and it shall be a new Jerusalem. And the powers of heaven shall be in the midst of this people; yea, even I will be in the midst of you.—III. *Nephi xx: 21-22.*

And they shall assist my people, the remnant of Jacob, and also, as many of the house of Israel as shall come, that they may build a city, which shall be called the New Jerusalem;

And then shall they assist my people that they may be gathered in, who are scattered upon all the face of the land, in unto the New Jerusalem.

And then shall the power of heaven come down among them; and I also will be in the midst.—*III. Nephi xxi: 23-25.*

Therefore more blessed are ye, for ye shall never taste of death, but ye shall live to behold all the doings of the Father, unto the children of men, even until all things shall be fulfilled, according to the will of the Father, when I shall come in my glory, with the powers of heaven.—*III. Nephi xxviii: 7.*

Christ to come to his temple.

And it came to pass that he commanded them that they should write the words which the Father had given unto

Malachi, which he should tell unto them. And it came to pass that after they were written, he expounded them. And these are the words which he did tell unto them, saying, Thus saith the Father unto Malachi, Behold I will send my messenger, and he shall prepare the way before me, and the Lord whom ye seek shall suddenly come to his temple, even the messenger of the covenant, whom ye delight in; behold, he shall come, saith the Lord of Hosts.

But who may abide the day of his coming? and who shall stand when he appeareth? for he is like unto a refiner's fire and like fuller's soap.

And he shall sit as a refiner and purifier of silver: and he shall purify the sons of Levi, and purge them as gold and silver, that they may offer unto the Lord an offering in righteousness.—*III. Nephi xxiv: 1-3.*

THE ATONEMENT.

And it came to pass that the Jews did mock him, because of the things which he testified of them; for he truly testified of their wickedness and their abominations; and he testified that the things which he saw and heard, and also the things which he read in the book, manifested plainly of the coming of a Messiah, and also the redemption of the world.—*I. Nephi i: 19.*

Lehi testifies of the Atonement.

Yea, even six hundred years from the time that my father left Jerusalem, a prophet would the Lord God raise up among the Jews, even a Messiah; or, in other words, a Savior of the world.

And he also spake concerning the prophets, how great a number had testified of these things, concerning this Messiah, of whom he had spoken, or this Redeemer of the world.

Wherefore all mankind were in a lost and in a fallen state, and ever would be, save they should rely on this Redeemer. —*I. Nephi x: 4-6.*

Nephi's vision of the Savior.

And it came to pass that I looked and beheld the great city of Jerusalem, and also other cities. And I beheld the city of Nazareth; and in the city of Nazareth I beheld a virgin, and she was exceedingly fair and white.

And it came to pass that I saw the heavens open; and an angel came down and stood before me; and he said unto me, Nephi, what beholdest thou?

And I said unto him, a virgin, most beautiful and fair above all other virgins.

And he said unto me, Behold the virgin whom thou seest, is the mother of the Son of God, after the manner of the flesh.

And it came to pass that I beheld that she was carried away in the Spirit; and after she had been carried away in the Spirit for the space of a time, the angel spake unto me, saying, Look!

And I looked and beheld the virgin again, bearing a child in her arms.

And the angel said unto me, Behold the Lamb of God, yea, even the Son of the Eternal Father! Knowest thou the meaning of the tree which thy father saw?

And I answered him saying, Yea, it is the love of God, which sheddeth itself abroad in the hearts of the children of men; wherefore, it is the most desirable above all things.

And he spake unto me again, saying, Look! And I looked, and I beheld the Lamb of God going forth among the children of men. And I beheld multitudes of people who were sick, and who were afflicted with all manner of diseases, and with devils, and unclean spirits; and the angel spake and showed all these things unto me. And they were healed by the power of the Lamb of God; and the devils and the unclean spirits were cast out.

And it came to pass that the angel spake unto me again, saying, Look! And I looked and beheld the Lamb of God, that he was taken by the people; yea, the Son of the everlasting God was judged of the world; and I saw and bear record.

And I, Nephi, saw that he was lifted up upon the cross, and slain for the sins of the world.—*I. Nephi xi: 13-15, 18-22, 31-33.*

Christ the
end of the
law.

Wherefore, redemption cometh in and through the Holy Messiah; for he is full of grace and truth.

Behold he offereth himself a sacrifice for sin, to answer the ends of the law, unto all those who have a broken heart and a contrite spirit; and unto none else can the ends of the law be answered.

Wherefore, how great the importance to make these things known unto the inhabitants of the earth, that they may know that there is no flesh that can dwell in the presence of God, save it be through the merits, and mercy, and grace of the Holy Messiah, who layeth down his life according to the flesh, and taketh it again by the power of the Spirit, that he may bring to pass the resurrection of the dead, being the first that should rise.—*Il. Nephi ii: 6-8.*

The
atonement
for original
sin uncon-
ditional.

And now, behold, if Adam had not transgressed, he would not have fallen; but he would have remained in the garden of Eden. And all things which were created, must have remained in the same state which they were after they were created; and they must have remained for ever, and had no end.

And they would have had no children; wherefore, they would have remained in a state of innocence; having no joy, for they knew no misery; doing no good, for they knew no sin.

But behold, all things have been done in the wisdom of him who knoweth all things.

Adam fell that men might be; and men are, that they might have joy.

And the Messiah cometh in the fulness of time, that he may redeem the children of men from the fall. And because that they are redeemed from the fall, they have become free for ever, knowing good from evil; to act for themselves, and not to be acted upon, save it be by the punishment of the law at the great and last day, according to the commandments which God hath given.—II. *Nephi ii: 22-26.*

Behold, he created Adam, and by Adam came the fall of man. And because of the fall of man, came Jesus Christ, even the Father and the Son; and because of Jesus Christ came the redemption of man.

The atonement for original sin unconditional.

" And because of the redemption of man, which came by Jesus Christ, they are brought back into the presence of the Lord; yea, this is wherein all men are redeemed, because the death of Christ bringeth to pass the resurrection, which bringeth to pass a redemption from an endless sleep, from which sleep all men shall be awoke by the power of God when the trump shall sound; and they shall come forth, both small and great, and all shall stand before his bar, being redeemed and loosed from this eternal band of death, which death is a temporal death.—*Mormon ix: 12-13.*

And thus we see that all mankind were fallen, and they were in the grasp of justice; yea, the justice of God, which consigned them for ever to be cut off from his presence.

And now the plan of mercy could not be brought about, except an atonement should be made; therefore God himself atoneth for the sins of the world, to bring about the plan of mercy, to appease the demands of justice, that God might be a perfect, just God, and a merciful God also.—*Alma xlii: 14-15.*

Application to personal sins conditional.

I say unto you, if ye have come to a knowledge of the goodness of God, and his matchless power, and his wisdom, and his patience, and his long suffering towards the children of men, and also the atonement which has been prepared from the foundation of the world, that thereby salvation might come to him that should put his trust in the Lord, and should be diligent in keeping his commandments, and continue in the faith even unto the end of his life; I mean the life of the mortal body;

I say, that this is the man who receiveth salvation, through the atonement which was prepared from the foundation of the world for all mankind, which ever were ever since the fall of Adam, or who are, or who ever shall be, even unto the end of the world.—*Mosiah iv: 6-7.*

And Aaron did expound unto him the scriptures, from the creation of Adam, laying the fall of man before him, and their carnal state and also the plan of redemption, which was prepared from the foundation of the world, through Christ, for all whosoever would believe on his name.

And since man had fallen, he could not merit anything of himself; but the sufferings and death of Christ, atoneth for their sins, through faith and repentance, &c.; and that he breaketh the bands of death, that the grave shall have no victory, and that the sting of death should be swallowed up in the hopes of glory: and Aaron did expound all these things unto the king.—*Alma xxii: 13-14.*

And he cometh into the world that he may save all men, if they will hearken unto his voice; for behold, he suffereth the pains of all men; yea, the pains of every living creature, both men, women, and children, who belong to the family of Adam.

Application to personal sins conditional.

Wherefore he has given a law; and where there is no law given, there is no punishment; and where there is no punishment, there is no condemnation; and where there is no condemnation, the mercies of the Holy One of Israel have claim upon them, because of the atonement; for they are delivered by the power of him;

For the atonement satisfieth the demands of his justice upon all those who have not the law given to them, that they are delivered from that awful monster, death and hell, and the devil, and the lake of fire and brimstone, which is endless torment; and they are restored to that God who gave them breath, which is the Holy One of Israel.

·But wo unto him that has the law given; yea, that has all the commandments of God like unto us, and that transgresseth them, and that wasteth the days of his probation, for awful is his state.—II. *Nephi ix: 21, 25-27.*

Christ sheweth himself unto the Nephites.

And it came to pass as they understood, they cast their eyes up again towards heaven; and behold, they saw a man descending out of heaven; and he was clothed in a white robe, and he came down and stood in the midst of them, and the eyes of the whole multitude were turned upon him, and they durst not open their mouths, even one to another, and wist not what it meant, for they thought it was an angel that had appeared unto them.

And it came to pass that he stretched forth his hand and spake unto the people, saying,

Behold, I am Jesus Christ, whom the prophets testified shall come into the world;

And behold, I am the light and the life of the world; and I have drunk out of that bitter cup which the Father hath given me, and have glorified the Father in taking upon me the sins of the world, in the which I have suffered the will of the Father in all things from the beginning.

And it came to pass that the Lord spake unto them saying,

Arise and come forth unto me, that ye may thrust your hands into my side, and also that ye may feel the print of the nails in my hands and in my feet, that ye may know that I am the God of Israel, and the God of the whole earth, and have been slain for the sins of the world.

And it came to pass that the multitude went forth, and thrust their hands into his side, ahd did feel the prints of the nails in his hands and in his feet; and this they did do, going forth one by one, until they had all gone forth, and did see with their eyes, and did feel with their hands, and did know of a surety, and did bear record, that it was he of whom it was written by the prophets that should come.—*III. Nephi xi*: *8-11, 13-15.*

PRE-EXISTENCE OF SPIRITS.

For behold, the time cometh, and is not far distant, that with power, the Lord Omnipotent who reigneth, who was, and is from all eternity to all eternity, shall come down from heaven, among the children of men, and shall dwell in a tabernacle of clay, and shall go forth amongst men, working mighty

Jesus Christ's pre-existence

miracles, such as healing the sick, rais-
ing the dead, causing the lamb to walk,
the blind to receive their sight, and the
deaf to hear, and curing all manner of
diseases;

Christ
created the
heavens and
the earth.

And he shall be called Jesus Christ,
the Son of God, the Father of heaven
and earth, the Creator of all things,
from the beginning; and his mother
shall be called Mary.—*Mosiah iii:* 5, 8.

And they had viewed themselves in
their own carnal state, even less than the
dust of the earth. And they all cried
with one voice, saying, O have mercy,
and apply the atoning blood of Christ,
that we may receive forgiveness of our
sins, and our hearts may be purified:
for we believe in Jesus Christ, the Son
of God, who created heaven and earth,
and all things; who shall come down
among the children of men.—*Mosiah iv:* 2.

The children
of Israel led
by Christ.

Behold I am Jesus Christ the Son of
God. I created the heavens and the
earth, and all things that in them are.
I was with the Father from the beginning.
I am in the Father, and the Father in
me; and in me hath the Father glorified
his name. —*III Nephi ix:* 15.

Now ye know that Moses was commanded of the Lord to do that great
work; and ye know that by his word,
the waters of the Red Sea divided hither
and thither, and they passed through on
dry ground.
And notwithstanding they being led,
the Lord their God, their Redeemer

going before them, leading them by day, and giving light unto them by night, and doing all things for them which were expedient for man to receive, they hardened their hearts, and blinded their minds, and reviled against Moses and against the true and living God.—*I. Nephi xvii: 26, 30.*

The Redeemer seen by Nephi and Jacob.

And now I, Nephi, write more of the words of Isaiah, for my soul delighteth in his words. For I will liken his words unto my people, and I will send them forth unto all my children, for he verily saw my Redeemer, even as I have seen him.

And my brother Jacob also has seen him as I have seen him: wherefore I will send their words forth unto my children, to prove unto them that my words are true. Wherefore, by the words of three, God hath said, I will establish my word. Nevertheless, God sendeth more witnesses, and he proveth all his words.—II. *Nephi xi: 2-3.*

Voice of the Lord heard on the night preceding His birth.

Now it came to pass that when Nephi, the son of Nephi, saw this wickedness of his people, his heart was exceeding sorrowful.

And it came to pass that he went out and bowed himself down upon the earth, and cried mightily to his God, in behalf of his people; yea, those who were about to be destroyed because of their faith in the tradition of their fathers.

And it came to pass that he cried mightily unto the Lord, all the day; and behold, the voice of the Lord came unto him, saying,

Lift up your head and be of good cheer, for behold, the time is at hand, and on this night shall the sign be given, and on the morrow come I into the world, to shew unto the world that I will fulfill all that which I have caused to be spoken by the mouth of my holy prophets.—*III. Nephi i: 10-13.*

Man's pre-existence.

Now concerning the state of the soul between death and the resurrection. Behold, it has been made known unto me, by an angel, that the spirits of all men, as soon as they are departed from this mortal body; yea, the spirits of all men, whether they be good or evil, are taken home to that God who gave them life.—*Alma xl: 11.*

Spirit of man immortal.

I say unto you, that I have caused that ye should assemble yourselves together, that I might rid my garments of your blood, at this period of time when I am about to go down to my grave, that I might go down in peace, and my immortal spirit may join the choirs above in singing the praises of a just God.—*Mosiah ii: 28.*

THE INTERMEDIATE STATE.

Now there must needs be a space betwixt the time of death, and the time of the resurrection.

And now I would inquire what becometh of the souls of men from this time of death, to the time appointed for the resurrection?

Now whether there is more than one time appointed for men to rise, it mattereth not; for all do not die at once: and this mattereth not; all is as one day, with God; and time only is measured unto men;

Therefore there is a time appointed unto men, that they shall rise from the dead; and there is a space between the time of death and the resurrection. And now concerning this space of time. What becometh of the souls of men, is the thing which I have enquired diligently of the Lord to know; and this is the thing of which I do know.

Now concerning the state of the soul between death and the resurrection. Behold, it has been made known unto me, by an angel, that the spirits of all men, as soon as they are departed from this mortal body; yea, the spirits of all men, whether they be good or evil, are taken home to that God who gave them life.

And then shall it come to pass that the spirits of those who are righteous

State of the soul between death and the resurrection.

are received into a state of happiness, which is called paradise; a state of rest; a state of peace, where they shall rest from all their troubles and from all care, and sorrow, &c.

And then shall it come to pass, that the spirits of the wicked, yea, who are evil; for behold, they have no part nor portion of the Spirit of the Lord; for behold, they chose evil works rather than good; therefore the spirit of the devil did enter into them, and take possession of their house; and these shall be cast out into outer darkness; there shall be weeping, and wailing, and gnashing of teeth; and this because of their own iniquity; being led captive by the will of the devil.

Now this is the state of the souls of the wicked; yea, in darkness, and a state of awful, fearful, looking for the fiery indignation of the wrath of God upon them; thus they remain in this state, as well as the righteous in paradise, until the time of their resurrection.—*Alma xl: 6-9, 11-14.*

State of the soul between death and he resurrection.

I say unto you, that I have caused that ye should assemble yourselves together, that I might rid my garments of your blood, at this period of time when I am about to go down to my grave, that I might go down in peace, and my immortal spirit may join the choirs above in singing the praises of a just God.—*Mosiah ii: 28.*

And this death of which I have spoken, which is the spiritual death, shall deliver up its dead; which spiritual death is hell; wherefore, death and hell must deliver up their dead, and hell must deliver up its captive spirits, and the grave must deliver up its captive bodies, and the bodies and the spirits of men will be restored one to the other; and it is by the power of the resurrection of the Holy One of Israel.

Paradise a place for departed spirits

O how great the plan of our God! For on the other hand, the paradise of God must deliver up the spirits of the righteous, and the grave deliver up the body of the righteous; and the spirit and the body is restored to itself again, and all men become incorruptible and immortal, and they are living souls, having a perfect knowledge like unto us in the flesh; save it be that our knowledge shall be perfect.—II. *Nephi ix: 12-13.*

And it came to pass that the seventy and first year passed away, and also the seventy and second year; yea, and in fine, till the seventy and ninth year had passed away; yea, even an hundred years had passed away, and the disciples of Jesus, whom he had chosen, had all gone to the paradise of God, save it were the three who should tarry; and there were other disciples ordained in their stead; and also many of that generation which had passed away. — *IV. Nephi i: 14.*

Paradise a place for departed spirits

And now I bid unto all, farewell. I soon go to rest in the paradise of God, until my spirit and my body shall again re-unite, and I am brought forth triumphant through the air, to meet you before the pleasing bar of the great Jehovah, the eternal Judge of both quick and dead. Amen.—*Moroni x: 34.*

SALVATION FOR THE DEAD.—REDEMPTION OF THOSE WHO DIE WITHOUT LAW.

Conditions of salvation.

For behold thus saith Jesus Christ, the Son of God, unto his disciples who should tarry; yea, and also to all his disciples, in the hearing of the multitude, Go ye into all the world, and preach the gospel to every creature,

And he that believeth and is baptized, shall be saved, but he that believeth not, shall be damned.—*Mormon ix: 22-23.*

And he commandeth all men that they must repent, and be baptized in his name, having perfect faith in the Holy One of Israel, or they cannot be saved in the kingdom of God.— *II. Nephi ix: 23.*

Mission of Elijah.

Behold, I will send you Elijah the prophet before the coming of the great and dreadful day of the Lord;

And he shall turn the heart of the fathers to the children, and the heart of the children to their fathers, lest I come and smite the earth with a curse.—*III. Nephi xxv: 5-6.*

Wherefore he has given a law; and where there is no law given, there is no punishment; and where there is no punishment, there is no condemnation; and where there is no condemnation, the mercies of the Holy One of Israel have claim upon them because of the atonement; for they are delivered by the power of him;

Where there is no law given there is no condemnation.

For the atonement satisfieth the demands of his justice upon all those who have not the law given to them, that they are delivered from that awful monster, death and hell, and the devil, and the lake of fire and brimstone, which is endless torment; and they are restored to that God who gave them breath, which is the Holy One of Israel.—*II. Nephi ix: 25-26.*

Yea, and I know that good and evil have come before all men; or he that knoweth not good from evil is blameless; but he that knoweth good and evil, to him it is given according to his desires; whether he desireth good or evil, life or death, joy or remorse of conscience.—*Alma xxix: 5.*

For behold, and also his blood atoneth for the sins of those who have fallen by the transgression of Adam, who have died, not knowing the will of God concerning them, or who have ignorantly sinned.—*Mosiah iii 11.*

For behold that all little children are alive in Christ, and also all they that are without the law. For the power of redemption cometh on all they that have no law; wherefore, he that is not condemned, or he that is under no condemnation, cannot repent; and unto such baptism availeth nothing.—*Moroni viii: 22.*

God remembereth the heathens;

And again, the Lord God hath commanded that men should not murder; that they should not lie; that they should not steal; that they should not take the name of the Lord their God in vain; that they should not envy; that they should not have malice; that they should not contend one with another; that they should not commit whoredoms; and that they should do none of these things; for whoso doeth them, shall perish;

For none of these iniquities come of the Lord; for he doeth that which is good among the children of men; and he doeth nothing save it be plain unto the children of men; and he inviteth them all to come unto him, and partake of his goodness; and he denieth none that come unto him, black and white, bond and free, male and female; and he remembereth the heathen, and all are alike unto God, both Jew and Gentile.— *II. Nephi xxvi: 32-33.*

They are redeemed by the Lord and have part in the first resurrection.

And these are those who have part in the first resurrection; and these are they that have died before Christ came in their ignorance, not having salvation declared unto them. And thus the Lord bringeth about the resurrection of these; and they have a part in the first resurrection, or have eternal life, being redeemed by the Lord.—*Mosiah xv: 24.*

THE RESURRECTION.

For as death hath passed upon all men, to fulfil the merciful plan of the great Creator, there must needs be a power of resurrection, and the resurrection must needs come unto man by reason of the fall; and the fall came by reason of transgression; and because man became fallen, they were cut off from the presence of the Lord.

And this death of which I have spoken, which is the spiritual death, shall deliver up its dead; which spiritual death is hell; wherefore, death and hell must deliver up their dead, and hell must deliver up its captive spirits, and the grave must deliver up its captive bodies, and the bodies and the spirits of men will be restored one to the other; and it is by the power of the resurrection of the Holy One of Israel.

O how great the plan of our God! For on the other hand, the paradise of God must deliver up the spirits of the right-

The resurrection universal.

eous, and the grave deliver up the body
of the righteous; and the spirit and the
body is restored to itself again, and all
men become incorruptible, and immortal,
and they are living souls, having a perfect knowledge like unto us in the flesh;
save it be that our knowledge shall be
perfect.

And he cometh into the world that he
may save all men, if they will hearken
unto his voice; for behold, he suffereth
the pains of all men; yea, the pains of
every living creature, both men, women,
and children, who belong to the family
of Adam.

And he suffereth this, that the resurrection might pass upon all men, that all
might stand before him at the great and
judgment day.—*II. Nephi ix: 6, 12-13,
21-22.*

**The
resurrection
universal.**

For behold, he surely must die, that
salvation may come; yea, it behoveth
him, and becometh expedient that he
dieth, to bring to pass the resurrection
of the dead, that thereby men may be
brought into the presence of the Lord;

Yea, behold this death bringeth to
pass the resurrection, and redeemeth
all mankind from the first death—that
spiritual death; for all mankind, by the
fall of Adam, being cut off from the
presence of the Lord, are considered as
dead, both as to things temporal and to
things spiritual.

But behold, the resurrection of Christ
redeemeth mankind, yea, even all man-

kind, and bringeth them back into the presence of the Lord.—*Helaman xiv: 15-17.*

Now, my son, here is somewhat more. I would say unto thee; for I perceive that thy mind is worried concerning the resurrection of the dead.

Christ the firstfruits of the resurrection.

Behold, I say unto you, that there is no resurrection; or, I would say, in other words, that this mortal does not put on immortality; this corruption does not put on incorruption, until after the coming of Christ.

And behold, again it hath been spoken, that there is a first resurrection; a resurrection of all those who have been, or who are, or who shall be, down to the resurrection of Christ from the dead.

Resurrection at the resurrection of Christ.

Now whether the souls and the bodies of those of whom have been spoken, shall all be re-united at once, the wicked as well as the righteous, I do not say; let it suffice, that I say that they all come forth; or in other words, their resurrection cometh to pass before the resurrection of those who die after the resurrection of Christ.

Now my son, I do not say that their resurrection cometh at the resurrection of Christ; but behold, I give it as my opinion, that the souls and the bodies are re-united, of the righteous, at the resurrection of Christ, and his ascension into heaven.

The soul shall be restored to the body, and the body to the soul; yea, and every limb and joint shall be restored to its body; yea, even a hair of the head shall not be lost, but all things shall be restored to their proper and perfect frame. —*Alma xl: 1-2, 16, 19-20, 23.*

Resurrection at the resurrection of Christ.

But behold, the bands of death shall be broken, and the Son reigneth, and hath power over the dead; therefore, he bringeth to pass the resurrection of the dead.

And there cometh a resurrection, even a first resurrection; yea, even a resurrection of those that have been, and who are, and who shall be, even until the resurrection of Christ; for so shall he be called.

And now, the resurrection of all the prophets, and all those that have believed in their words, or all those that have kept the commandments of God, shall come forth in the first resurrection; therefore, they are the first resurrection.

They are raised to dwell with God who has redeemed them: thus they have eternal life through Christ, who has broken the bands of death.

And these are those who have part in the first resurrection; and these are they that have died before Christ came in their ignorance, not having salvation declared unto them. And thus the Lord bringeth about the restoration of these; and they have a part in the first resurrection, or have eternal life, being redeemed by the Lord.—*Mosiah xv: 20-24.*

And it came to pass as they understood, they cast their eyes up again towards heaven; and behold, they saw a
man descending out of heaven; and he
was clothed in a white robe, and he
came down and stood in the midst of
them, and the eyes of the whole multitude were turned upon him, and they
durst not open their mouths, even one
to another, and wist not what it meant,
for they thought it was an angel that
had appeared unto them.

And it came to pass that he stretched
forth his hand and spake unto the people,
saying,

Behold, I am Jesus Christ, whom the
prophets testified shall come into the
world;

And behold, I am the light and the
life of the world; and I have drunk out
of that bitter cup which the Father hath
given me, and have glorified the Father
in taking upon me the sins of the world,
in the which I have suffered the will of
the Father in all things from the beginning.

And it came to pass that the Lord
spake unto them saying,

Arise and come forth unto me, that
ye may thrust your hands into my side,
and also that ye may feel the print of
the nails in my hands and in my feet,
that ye may know that I am the God of
Israel, and the God of the whole earth,
and have been slain for the sins of the
world.

And it came to pass that the multi-

Christ shew-
eth himself
unto the
Nephites
after his
resurrection.

tude went forth, and thrust their hands
into his side, and did feel the prints
of the nails in his hands and in his feet;
and this they did do, going forth one by
one, until they had all gone forth, and
did see with their eyes, and did feel
with their hands, and did know of a
surety, and did bear record, that it was
he of whom it was written by the prophets that should come.—*III. Nephi xi*:
8-11, 13-15.

Saints did
arise.

And it came to pass that he said unto
Nephi, bring forth the record which ye
have kept.

And when Nephi had brought forth
the records and laid them before him,
he cast his eyes upon them and said,

Verily I say unto you, I commanded
my servant Samuel, the Lamanite, that
he should testify unto this people, that
at the day that the Father should glorify
his name in me, that there were many
saints who should arise from the dead,
and should appear unto many, and
should minister unto them. And he said
unto them, were it not so?

And his disciples answered him and
said, Yea, Lord, Samuel did prophesy
according to thy words, and they were
all fulfilled.

And Jesus said unto them, How be it
that ye have not written this thing, that
many saints did arise and appear unto
many, and did minister unto them?

And it came to pass that Jesus com-

manded that it should be written; therefore it was written according as he
commanded.—*III. Nephi xxiii: 7-11, 13.*

And there were great and marvelous
works wrought by the disciples of Jesus,
insomuch that they did heal the sick,
and raise the dead, and cause the lame
to walk, and the blind to receive sight,
and the deaf to hear; and all manner of
miracles did they work among the children of men; and in nothing did they
work miracles save it were in the name
of Jesus.—*IV. Nephi i: 5.*

Disciples raise the dead.

And because of the redemption of man,
which came by Jesus Christ, they are
brought back into the presence of the
Lord; yea, this is wherein all men are
redeemed, because the death of Christ
bringeth to pass the resurrection, which
bringeth to pass a redemption from an
endless sleep, from which sleep all men
shall be awoke by the power of God
when the trump shall sound; and they
shall come forth, both small and great,
and all shall stand before his bar, being
redeemed and loosed from this eternal
band of death, which death is a temporal
death;

Judgment to follow the resurrection.

And then cometh the judgment of the
Holy One upon them, and then cometh
the time that he that is filthy shall be
filthy still; and he that is righteous, shall
be righteous still; he that is happy shall
be happy still; and he that is unhappy
shall be unhappy still.—*Mormon ix: 13-14*

But whether it be at his resurrection,
or after, I do not say; but this much I
say, that there is a space between death
and the resurrection of the body, and a
state of the soul in happiness or in
misery until the time which is appointed
of God that the dead shall come forth,
and be re-united, both soul and body,
and be brought to stand before God, and
be judged according to their works.—
Alma xl: 21.

Therefore the wicked remain as though
there had been no redemption made,
except it be the loosing of the bands of
death; for behold, the day cometh that
all shall rise from the dead and stand
before God, and be judged according to
their works.—*Alma xi: 41.*

PERSONALITY OF GOD.

Lehi's vision
And it came to pass that he returned
to his own house at Jerusalem; and he
cast himself upon his bed, being overcome with the Spirit and the things
which he had seen;

And being thus overcome with the
Spirit, he was carried away in a vision,
even that he saw the heavens open, and
he thought he saw God sitting upon his
throne, surrounded with numberless
concourses of angels in the attitude of
singing and praising their God.—*I.
Nephi i: 7-8.*

And because he said unto them, That Christ was the God, the Father of all things, and said that he should take upon him the image of man, and it should be the image after which man was created in the beginning; or in other words, he said that man was created after the image of God, and that God should come down among the children of men, and take upon him flesh and blood, and go forth upon the face of the earth.—*Mosiah vii: 27.*

Ammon said unto him, I am a man; and man in the beginning was created after the image of God, and I am called by his Holy Spirit to teach these things unto this people, that they may be brought to a knowledge of that which is just and true.—*Alma xviii: 34.*

And it came to pass that when Aaron saw that the king would believe his words, he began from the creation of Adam, reading the scriptures unto the king: how God created man after his own image, and that God gave him commandments, and that because of transgression man had fallen.—*Alma xxii: 12.*

And I know, O Lord, that thou hast all power, and can do whatsoever thou wilt for the benefit of man; therefore touch these stones, O Lord, with thy finger, and prepare them that they may shine forth in darkness, and they shall shine forth unto us in the vessels which we have prepared, that we may have light while we shall cross the sea.

Marginal notes:
Man created in the image of God.

Jared's brother saw the Lord.

And it came to pass that when the brother of Jared had said these words, behold, the Lord stretched forth his hand and touched the stones, one by one with his finger; and the vail was taken from off the eyes of the brother of Jared, and he saw the finger of the Lord; and it was as the finger of a man, like unto flesh and blood; and the brother of Jared fell down before the Lord, for he was struck with fear.

And the Lord saw that the brother of Jared had fallen to the earth; and the Lord said unto him, Arise, why hast thou fallen?

And he saith unto the Lord, I saw the finger of the Lord, and I feared lest he should smite me; for I knew not that the Lord had flesh and blood.

And when he had said these words, behold, the Lord shewed himself unto him, and said, Because thou knowest these things, ye are redeemed from the fall; therefore ye are brought back into my presence; therefore I shew myself unto you.

And never have I shewed myself unto man whom I have created, for never has man believed in me as thou hast. Seest thou that ye are created after mine own image? Yea, even all men were created in the beginning, after mine own image.— *Ether iii: 4, 6-8, 13, 15.*

Attributes of Deity.

Now have we not reason to rejoice? Yea, I say unto you, there never were men that had so great reason to rejoice as we, since the world began; yea, and my joy is carried away, even unto the boasting in my God; for he has all power, all wisdom, ahd all understanding; he comprehendeth all things, and he is a merciful Being, even unto salvation, to those who will repent and believe on his name.—*Alma xxvi: 35.*

TITHING.

Even from the days of your fathers ye are gone away from mine ordinances, and have not kept them. Return unto me and I will return unto you, saith the Lord of Hosts. But ye said, wherein shall we return?

Will a man rob God? Yet ye have robbed me. But ye say, wherein have we robbed thee? In tithes and offerings.

Ye are cursed with a curse, for ye have robbed me, even this whole nation. Bring ye all the tithes into the storehouse, that there may be meat in my house; and prove me now herewith, saith the Lord of Hosts, if I will not open you the windows of heaven, and pour you out a blessing, that there shall not be room enough to receive it.

And I will rebuke the devourer for your sakes, and he shall not destroy the fruits of your ground; neither shall your vine cast her fruit before the time in the fields, saith the Lord of Hosts.

And all nations shall call you blessed,

Blessings promised to those who pay tithes.

for ye shall be a delightsome land, saith the Lord of Hosts —*III. Nephi xxiv: 7-12.*

Abraham paid tithes to Melchizedek

And now, my brethren, I would that ye should humble yourselves before God, and bring forth fruit meet for repentance, that ye may also enter into that rest;

Yea, humble yourselves even as the people in the days of Melchizedek, who was also a High Priest after this same order which I have spoken, who also took upon him the High Priesthood for ever.

And it was the same Melchizedek to whom Abraham paid tithes; yea, even our father Abraham paid tithes of onetenth part of all he possessed.—*Alma xiii: 13-15.*

THE UNITED ORDER.

All things common.

And it came to pass that the disciples whom Jesus had chosed, began from that time forth to baptize and to teach as many as did come unto them; and as many as were baptized in the name of Jesus, were filled with the Holy Ghost.

And they taught, and did minister one to another; and they had all things common among them, every man dealing justly, one with another.—*III. Nephi xxvi: 17, 19.*

And it came to pass in the thirty and sixth year, the people were all converted unto the Lord, upon all the face of the land, both Nephites and Lamanites, and there were no contentions and disputations among them, and every man did deal justly one with another;

The United Order observed by all the people.

And they had all things common among them, therefore they were not rich and poor, bond and free, but they were all made free, and partakers of the heavenly gift.—*IV. Nephi i: 2-3.*

And now in this two hundred and first year, there began to be among them those who were lifted up in pride, such as the wearing of costly apparel, and all manner of fine pearls, and of the fine things of the world.

The Order broken up.

And from that time forth they did have their goods and their substance no more common among them.—*IV. Nephi i: 24-25.*

LATTER-DAY REVELATION.

For Joseph truly testified, saying: A seer shall the Lord my God raise up, who shall be a choice seer unto the fruit of my loins.

A Seer to be raised up.

And his name shall be called after me: and it shall be after the name of his father. And he shall be like unto me; for the thing which the Lord shall bring forth by his hand, by the power of the Lord shall bring my people unto salvation.—*II. Nephi iii: 6, 15.*

A Book to come out of the earth.

But behold, I prophesy unto you concerning the last days; concerning the days when the Lord God shall bring these things forth unto the children of men.—*II. Nephi xxvi: 14.*

And it shall come to pass, that the Lord God shall bring forth unto you the words of a book, and they shall be the words of them which have slumbered.

And behold the book shall be sealed: and in the book shall be a revelation from God, from the beginning of the world to the ending thereof.—*II. Nephi xxvii: 6-7.*

And blessed be him that shall bring this thing to light: for it shall be brought out of darkness unto light, according to the word of God; yea, it shall be brought out of the earth, and it shall shine forth out of darkness, and come unto the knowledge of the people; and it shall be done by the power of God.—*Mormon viii: 16.*

Other books.

And after it had come forth unto them, I beheld other books, which came forth by the power of the Lamb, from the Gentiles unto them, unto the convincing of the Gentiles, and the remnant of the seed of my brethren, and also the Jews, who were scattered upon all the face of the earth, that the records of the prophets and of the twelve apostles of the Lamb are true.—*I. Nephi xiii: 39.*

And it came to pass that he commanded them that they should write the words which the Father had given unto Malachi, which he should tell unto them. And it came to pass that after they were written, he expounded them. And these are the words which he did tell unto them, saying, Thus said the Father unto Malachi, Behold, I will send my messenger, and he shall prepare the way before me, and the Lord whom ye seek shall suddenly come to his temple, even the messenger of the covenant, whom ye delight in; behold, he shall come, saith the Lord of Hosts. — *III. Nephi xxiv: 1.*

A heavenly messenger promised.

Behold, I will send you Elijah the prophet before the coming of the great and dreadful day of the Lord;
And he shall turn the heart of the fathers to the children, and the heart of the children to their fathers, lest I come and smite the earth with a curse.—III. *Nephi xxv: 5-6.*

Elijah to come.

Behold, I was about to write the names of those who were never to taste of death; but the Lord forbade, therefore I write them not, for they are hid from the world.
But behold I have seen them, and they have ministered unto me;
And behold they will be among the Gentiles, and the Gentiles knoweth them not.
They will also be among the Jews, and the Jews shall know them not.
And it shall come to pass, when the

Three disciples to minister.

Lord seeth fit in his wisdom, that they shall minister unto all the scattered tribes of Israel, and unto all nations, kindreds, tongues and people, and shall bring out of them unto Jesus many souls, that their desire may be fulfilled, and also because of the convincing power of God which is in them;

·And they are as the angels of God, and if they shall pray unto the Father in the name of Jesus, they can show themselves unto whatsoever man it seemeth them good;

Therefore great and marvellous works shall be wrought by them, before the great and coming day, when all people must surely stand before the judgment seat of Christ;

Yea, even among the Gentiles shall there be a great and marvellous work wrought by them, before that judgment day.—*III. Nephi xxviii: 25-32.*

A Lamanite Prophet to arise.

And there shall rise up one mighty among them, who shall do much good, both in word and in deed, being an instrument in the hands of God, with exceeding faith, to work mighty wonders, and do that thing which is great in the sight of God, unto the bringing to pass much restoration unto the house of Israel, and unto the seed of thy brethren.—*II. Nephi iii: 24.*

More revelation promised.

For behold, thus saith the Lord God, I will give unto the children of men line upon line, precept upon precept, here a little and there a little; and blessed are those who hearken unto my precepts, and lend an ear unto my counsel, for they shall learn wisdom; for unto him that receiveth, I will give more; and from them that shall say, We have enough, from them shall be taken away even that which they have.—*II. Nephi xxviii: 30.*

And when they shall have received this, which is expedient that they should have first, to try their faith, and if it shall so be that they shall believe these things, then shall the greater things be made ·manifest. unto them.—*III. Nephi xxvi: 9.*

More revelation promised.

For the Lord said unto me, They shall not go forth unto the Gentiles until the day that they shall repent of their iniquity, and become clean before the Lord;

And in that day that they shall exercise faith in me, saith the Lord, even as the brother of Jared did, that they may become sanctified in me, then will I manifest unto them the things which the brother of Jared saw, even to the unfolding unto them all my revelations, saith Jesus Christ, the Son of God, the Father of the heavens and of the earth, and all things that in them are.—*Ether iv: 6-7.*

PERSECUTION,

THE HERITAGE OF THE FAITHFUL.

Lehi perse-
cuted by the
Jews.

Therefore, I would that ye should know, that after the Lord had shown so many marvellous things unto my father, Lehi, yea, concerning the destruction of Jerusalem, behold he went forth among the people, and began to prophesy and to declare unto them concerning the things which he had both seen and heard.

And when the Jews heard these things, they were angry with him; yea, even as with the prophets of old, whom they had cast out and stoned, and slain; and they also sought his life, that they might take it away. But behold, I, Nephi, will shew unto you that the tender mercies of the Lord are over all those whom he has chosen, because of their faith, to make them mighty even unto the power of deliverance.—*I. Nephi i: 18, 20.*

Nephi and
Sam beaten.

And it came to pass that Laman was angry with me, and also with my father; and also was Lemuel; for he hearkened unto the words of Laman. Wherefore Laman and Lemuel did speak many hard words unto us, their younger brothers, and they did smite us even with a rod.—*1. Nephi iii: 28.*

Abinadi
scourged
with faggots

And now it came to pass that when Abinadi had finished these sayings, that the king commanded that the priests should take him and cause that he should be put to death.

And it came to pass that they took him, and scourged his skin with faggots, yea, even unto death. —*Mosiah xvii: 1, 13.*

And it came to pass that he began to cry unto the people, saying: Behold, I am guilty, and these men are spotless before God. And he began to plead for them, from that time forth; but they reviled him, saying: Art thou also possessed with the devil? And they spit upon him, and cast him out trom among them, and also all those who believed in the words which had been spoken by Alma and Amulek; and they cast them out, and sent men to cast stones at them.

Believers stoned.

And they brought their wives and children together, and whosoever believed or had been taught to believe in the word of God, they caused that they should be cast into the fire; and they also brought forth their records which contained the Holy Scriptures, and cast them into the fire also, that they might be burned and destroyed by fire.—*Alma xiv: 7-8.*

Women and children cast into the fire.

Now when the people saw that they were coming against them, they went out to meet them, and prostrated themselves before them to the earth, and began to call on the name of the Lord; and thus they were in this attitude when the Lamanites began to fall upon them, and began to slay them with the sword;

A thousand and five massacred.

And thus without meeting any resistance, they did slay a thousand and five of them; and we know that they are blessed, for they have gone to dwell with their God.—*Alma xxiv: 21 22.*

Disciples cast into prison.

And we have entered into their houses and taught them, and we have taught them in their streets; yea, and we have taught them upon their hills; and we have also entered into their temples and their synagogues and taught them; and we have been cast out, and mocked, and spit upon, and smote upon our cheeks; and we have been stoned, and taken and bound with strong cords, and cast into prison; and through the power and wisdom of God we have been delivered again;

And we have suffered all manner of afflictions, and all this, that perhaps we might be the means of saving some soul, and we supposed that our joy would be full, if perhaps we could be the means of saving some.—*Alma xxvi: 29-30.*

Words of the Savior.

And blessed are all they who are persecuted for my name's sake, for theirs is the kingdom of heaven.

And blessed are ye when men shall revile you, and persecute and shall say all manner of evil against you falsely, for my sake,

For ye shall have great joy and be exceeding glad, for great shall be your reward in heaven; for so persecuted they the prophets who were before you.—*III. Nephi xii: 10-12.*

DOOM OF APOSTATES.

But, behold, my beloved brethren, thus came the voice of the Son unto me, saying, After ye have repented of your sins, and witnessed unto the Father that ye are willing to keep my commandments, by the baptism of water, and have received the baptism of fire and of the Holy Ghost, and can speak with a new tongue, yea, even with the tongue of angels, and after this should deny me, it would have been better for you that ye had not known me.—*II. Nephi xxxi: 14.*

Hopeless condition of apostates.

: And thus we can plainly discern, that after a people have been once enlightened by the Spirit of God, and have had great knowledge of things pertaining to righteousness, and then have fallen away into sin and transgression, they become more hardened, and thus their state becomes worse thah though they had never known these things.—*Alma xxiv: 30.*

And now, I say unto you, my brethren, that after ye have known and have been taught all these things, if ye should transgress, and go contrary to that which has been spoken, that ye do withdraw yourselves from the Spirit of the Lord, that it may have no place in you to guide you in wisdom's paths, that ye may be blessed, prospered, and preserved.

Final doom of apostates.

I say unto you, that the man that doeth this, the same cometh out in open re-

bellion against God; therefore he listeth
to obey the evil spirit, and becometh an
enemy to all righteousness; therefore,
the Lord has no place in him, for he
dwelleth not in unholy temples.

Therefore if that man repenteth not,
and remaineth and dieth an enemy to
God, the demands of divine justice doth
awaken his immortal soul to a lively
sense of his own guilt, which doth cause
him to shrink from the presence of the
Lord, and doth fill his breast with guilt,
and pain, and anguish, which is like an
unquenchable fire, whose flame ascendeth
up for ever and ever.

And now I say unto you, that mercy
hath no claim on that man; therefore,
his final doom is to endure a never ending torment.—*Mosiah ii: 36-39.*

LATTER-DAY JUDGMENTS.

Judgments
to be poured
out upon all
nations.

Wherefore, I write unto my people,
unto all those that shall receive hereafter
these things which I write, that they
may know the judgments of God, that
they come upon all nations, according to
the word which he hath spoken.—*II.
Nephi xxv: 3.*

But, behold, in the last days, or in the
days of the Gentiles; yea, behold all the
nations of the Gentiles, and also the
Jews, both those who shall come upon
this land, and those who shall be upon

other lands; yea, even upon all the lands of the earth; behold, they will be drunken with iniquity, and all manner of abominations;

And when that day shall come, they shall be visited of the Lord of Hosts, with thunder, and with earthquake, and with a great noise, and with storm, and with tempest, and with the flame of devouring fire;

And all the nations that fight against Zion, and that distress her, shall be as a dream of a night vision; yea, it shall be unto them, even as unto a hungry man, which dreameth, and behold he eateth, but he awaketh, and his soul is empty; or like unto a thirsty man, which dreameth, and behold he drinketh, but he awaketh, and behold he is faint, and his soul hath appetite; yea, even so shall the multitude of all the nations be that fight against Mount Zion.—*II. Nephi xxvii: 1-3.*

Wherefore, they that fight against Zion and the covenant people of the Lord, shall lick up the dust of their feet; and the people of the Lord shall not be ashamed. For the people of the Lord are they who wait for him; for they still wait for the coming of the Messiah.

And they that believe not in him, shall be destroyed, both by fire, and by tempest, and by earthquakes, and by bloodsheds, and by pestilence, and by famine. And they shall know that the

Judgments to overtake the enemies of Zion.

Lord is God, the Holy One of Israel.—
II. Nephi vi: 13, 15.

Latter-day Judgments. For it shall come to pass saith the Father, that at that day whosoever will not repent and come unto my beloved Son, them will I cut off from among my people, O house of Israel;

And I will execute vengeance and fury upon them, even as upon the heathen, such as they have not heard.—*III. Nephi xxi: 20-21.*

For behold, the day cometh that shall burn as an oven; and all the proud, yea, all that do wickedly, shall be stubble: and the day that cometh shall burn them up, saith the Lord of Hosts, that it shall leave them neither root nor branch.—*III. Nephi xxv: 1.*

THE NEW JERUSALEM.

Prophecy of Ether concerning a New Jerusalem Behold, Ether saw the days of Christ; and he spake concerning a New Jerusalem upon this land;

And that a New Jerusalem should be built up upon this land, unto the remnant of the seed of Joseph, for which things there has been a type;

To be built on the land of North America. Wherefore the remnant of the house of Joseph shall be built upon this land; and it shall be a land of their inheritance; and they shall build up a holy city unto the Lord, like unto the Jerusalem of old; and they shall no more be confounded, until the end come, when the earth shall pass away.—*Ether xiii*: *4, 6, 8.*

And behold, this people will I establish in this land, unto the fullfilling of the covenant which I made with your father Jacob; and it shall be a New Jerusalem. And the powers of heaven shall be in the midst of this people; yea, even I will be in the midst of you.—*III. Nephi xx*: *22.*

> The New Jerusalem referred to by Jesus.

But if they will repent, and hearken unto my words, and harden not their hearts, I will establish my church among them, and they shall come in unto the covenant, and be numbered among this the remnant of Jacob, unto whom I have given this land for their inheritance,

And they shall assist my people, the remnant of Jacob, and also, as many of the house of Israel as shall come, that they may build a city, which shall be called the New Jerusalem;

And then shall they assist my people that they may be gathered in, who are scattered upon all the face of the land, in unto the New Jerusalem.—*III. Nephi xxi: 22-24.*

TRADITIONS AND DISCOVERIES CONFIRMING THE BOOK OF MORMON.

The Jaredites, who came to America from the Tower of Babel. "So the Lord scattered them abroad from thence upon the face of all the earth; and they left off to build the city. Therefore is the name of it called Babel; because the Lord did there confound the language of all the earth: and from thence did the Lord scatter them abroad upon the face of the earth."—*Genesis xi: 8-9.*

" This historical item carries us back in our researches, according to Bible chronology, four thousand one hundred and twenty-seven years; a date beyond that which the scientists of our age have been able to definitely fix the first inhabiting of these continents. By it we not only learn that the Lord did confound the language of the people at the tower of Babel, but that he also scattered them abroad upon the face of *all* the earth. Now, how could this be accomplished without scattering some of them upon the Western Hemisphere, as well as others upon the Eastern? Was not the former, at that date of the world's history, a part of the face of *all* the earth, as well as the latter? A supposition that it was not, would be so weak and inconsistent, so utterly opposed to reason, as well as to the developments of science, that it must fail to find among the thoughtful either support or credence."—*Contributor Vol. ii, p. 197.*

" And now I, Moorni, proceed to give an account of those ancient inhabitants who were destroyed by the hand of the Lord upon the face of this north country (North America).

And I take mine account from the twenty and four plates which were found by the people of Limhi, which is called the book of Ether. And as I suppose that the first part of this record, which speaks concerning the creation of the world, and also of Adam, and an account from that time even to the great tower (Babel), and whatsoever things transpired among the children of men until that time, is had among the Jews; therefore I do not write those things which transpired from the days of Adam until that time; but they are had upon the plates, and whoso findeth them, the same will have power that he may get the full account."—*Ether i: 1-4.* "Which Jared came forth with his brother and their families, with some others and their families, from the great tower, at the time the Lord confounded the language of the people, and swear in his wrath that they should be scattered upon all the face of the earth; and according to the word of the Lord the people were scattered."—*Ether 1: 33.*

"Here, then, we find the inspired record of the historian Moses, written upon the Eastern Hemisphere, confirmed by the no less inspired writings of the historian Ether, who wrote nearly twenty-five hundred years ago upon the Western Hemisphere; bearing testimony, not only of the creation, but of the fact of his forefathers having been brought to America from the tower at the time the Lord confused the language of all the earth."—*Contributor Vol. ii, p. 197.*

Boturini, on page six of his work, says:—"There is no Gentile nation that refers to primitive events with such certainty as the Indians do. They give us an account of the creation of the world, of the deluge, of the confusion of languages at the Tower of Babel and of all other periods and ages of the world, and of the long peregrinations which their people had in Asia, representing the specific years by their characters; and in the Seven Conejos (rabbits) they tell us of the great eclipse that occurred at the death of Christ our Lord."

Prof. Short in his "North America of Antiquity," page two hundred and two, says: "That the American population is of old world origin there can be but little doubt; but from whence it came, and to what particular people or peoples it owes its birth, is quite another question."

"The era of their existence as a distinct and isolated race must probably be dated as far back as that time, which separated into nations the inhabitants of the old world, and gave to each branch of the human family its primitive language and individuality."—*Pritchard's National History of Man, London, 1845.*

"The native Mexican author, Ixtlilxochitl, fixes the date of the peopling of America about the year 2000 B. C., which closely accords with that given by the Book of Mormon, which positively declares that it occurred at the time of the dispersion, when God in His anger scattered the people from Babel upon the face of the whole earth."—*Contributor Vol. ii, p. 227.*

(For further information upon this subject, see "Divine Origin of the Book of Mormon," by Moses Thatcher, *Contributor Vol. ii, pp. 257-261.*)

Number of Vessels.   "And it came to pass that the brother of Jared, (now the number of the vessels which had been prepared was eight,) went forth unto the mount, which they called the mount Shelem, because of its exceeding height, and did moulten out of a rock sixteen small stones; and they were white and clear, even as transparent glass; and he did carry them in his hands upon the top of the mount."—*Ether 3: 1.*

"Don Francisco Munoz de la Vega, the Bishop of that diocese (Chiapa), certifies in the prologue to his 'Diocesan Constitutions,' declaring that an ancient manuscript of the primitive Indians of that province, who had learned the art of writing, was in his record office, who retained the constant tradition that the father and founder of their nation was named Teponahuale, which signifies the lord of the hollow piece of wood, and that he was present at the building of the Great Wall, for so they named the Tower of Babel, and beheld with his own eyes the confusion of language; after which event, God, the Creator, commanded him to come to these extensive regions, and to divide them amongst mankind.   They affirm that at the time of the confusion of tongues, there were SEVEN families who spoke the same language, which was Nahuatl, that which is still spoken by the Mexicans Aztecs), and since they understood each other, they united, and, forming a single company, proceeded on their journey, through divers lands and countries as chance directed them, and without any particular destination, in search of a convenient habitation; and having traveled during a century (which amongst them was a period of time amounting to one hundred and four years', passing in the interval, mountains, rivers and arms of the sea, which they noted down in their paintings, they arrived at the place where they made their first settlement, in the northern part of this kingdom, which they named Tlapalan, which signifies the red country, on account of the soil being of that color; and even still, in all modern maps (picture writings), they gave the name of the Red Sea to the gulf which is situated between the eastern coast of the province of New Mexico and Sonora; and the river (Colorado) which flows into the northern part of the gulf is named the Red River."—*Kingsborough's Mexican Antiquities, Vol. viii, pp. 25, 27.*

Clavigero says: "The Chiapanese have been the first peoplers of the New World, if we give credit to their traditions.   They say that Votan, the grandson of that respectable old man who built the great ark to save himself and family from the deluge, and one of those who undertook the building of that lofty edifice, which was to reach up to heaven, went by express command of the Lord to people that land.   They say also that the first people came from the quarter of the north, and that when they arrived at Soconusco, they separated, some going to inhabit the country of Nicaragua and others remaining at Chiapas."

"According to this tradition, Votan came from the East, from Valum Chivim, by way of Valum Votan, from across the sea, by divine command, to apportion the land of the new continent to SEVEN families which he brought with him."

"The Toltecs, consisting of SEVEN friends, with their wives, who understood the same language, came to these parts, having first passed great land and seas, having lived in caves, and having endured great hardships in order to reach this land; * * * they wandered one hundred and four years through different parts of the world before they reached Hue Hue Tlapalan, which was in Ce Tecpatl, five hundred and twenty years after the flood."—"*Ixtlilxochitl Relaciones,*" in *Kingsborough's* "*Mex. Ant.*" *Vol. ix, p. 322.*

"Josephus says that Nimrod was a mighty man, the grandson of Ham; the Book of Mormon speaks of the brother of Jared and his companions going down into a valley of that name called after the mighty hunter. Josephus speaks of ships in which some crossed over the sea, when God scattered the people everywhere from the Tower, and led them whithersoever He willed. We have seen that the colony of Jared's brother used EIGHT barges or vessels in which to cross the great deep. Most writers on American antiquities say SEVEN, but the historian, Francisco Espinosa, states the number as being EIGHT."

"Kingsborough states that the manuscript of the primitive Indians refers to the Tower as the 'Great Wall,' which the lord of the 'hollow piece of wood' saw, when it was being built, and beheld with his own eyes the confusion of the language of the people. Votan, it is stated, was a grandson of Noah, and came by express command of the Lord to the people of this land. The brother of Jared did the same; pleading with the Lord not to confound the language of Jared, or their friends and families. The seven families, being the same, doubtless, whom Votan led, maintained one language, being not confounded. They formed one company and traveled together many years (104), over rivers, mountains and arms of the sea. So did the colony led by Jared's brother, who was in the wilderness many year and built barges to cross many waters. If the records of the Indians, which survived the vandalism of the Roman Catholic clergy, who followed in the wake of the Spanish conquerors, are reliable, and form, when combined with the traditions of the primitive inhabitants of the land, a chain of facts like those produced even thus far, then who can consistently deny the divine origin of the Book of Mormon."—*Thatcher, in Contributor, Vol. ii.*

Jared's Brother Got Light for the Vessels. "And it came to pass that the brother of Jared, (now the number of the vessels which had been prepared was eight,) went forth unto the mount, which they called the mount of Shelem, because of its exceeding height, and did moulten out of a rock sixteen small stones; and they were white and clear, even as transparent glass; and he did carry them in his hands upon the top of the mount, and cried again unto the Lord, saying, * * * And I know, O Lord, that thou hast all power, and can do whatsoever thou wilt for the benefit of man; therefore touch these stones, O, Lord, with thy finger, and prepare them that they may shine forth in darkness; and they shall shine forth unto us in the vessels which we have prepared, that we may have light while we shall cross the sea.   * * *   And it came to pass that when the brother of Jared had said these words, behold, the Lord stretched forth his hand and touched the stones, one by one with his finger; and the vail was taken from off the eyes of the brother of Jared, and he saw the finger of the Lord; and it was as the finger of a man, like unto flesh and blood; and the brother of Jared fell down before the Lord, for he was struck with fear."—*Ether iii: 1, 4-6.*

"Montesinos tells us that at some time near the date of the Deluge, in other words, in the highest antiquity, America was invaded by a people with four leaders, named Ayar-mancotopa, Ayar-chaki, Ayar-aucca, and Ayar uyssu. 'Ayar,' says Senor Lopez, 'is the Sancrit *Ajar*, or *aje*, and means primitive chief; and *manco, chaki, aucca*, and *uyssu*, mean believers, wanderers, soldiers, husbandmen. We have here a tradition of castes like that preserved in the four tribal names of Athens.' The laboring class (naturally enough in a new colony) obtained the supremacy, and its leader was named Pirhua-manco, REVEALER OF PIR, LIGHT."—*Donnelly's Atlantis, p. 391. (Harper & Brothers, 1882.)*

Jared's Brother Moved a Mountain.   "For the Brother of Jared said unto the Mountain Zerin, remove, and it was removed. And if he had not had faith, it would not have moved; wherefore thou workest after men have faith."—*Ether xii: 30.*

Same, the great name of Brazilian legend, came across the ocean *from the rising sun.* He had power over the elements and tempests ; the trees of the forests would recede to make room for him; the animals used to crouch before him; lakes and rivers became solid for him; and he taught the use of agriculture and magic."—*Atlantis, p. 168.*

Art of Making Glass Known to the Jaredites.   "And it came to pass that the brother of Jared * * * did moulten out of a rock sixteen small stones; and they were white and clear, even as transparent glass."—*Ether iii: 1.*

Parts of a Glass Vase Found.   In 1880 the workmen of Desire Charnay, while exhuming the ruins of some extensive buildings at the ancient Metropolis of the Toltecs, situated about sixty-five miles to the north of the city of Mexico, discovered specimens of porcelain beautifully enameled, and parts of a GLASS VASE. Alluding to the discovery of the piece of glass, Mr. Charnay says:

"On this subject, I make no comments, yet I will add that nations are like individuals; they always esteem themselves more highly civilized than their predecessors. The Chinese, the Hindoos, the Egyptians, have left to us evidence of their genius: they understood the making of glass and of porcelain, and many other arts before we did, and to me, it is no matter of surprise that an intelligent population such as the Toltecs should have been able to erect monuments, to cut stone, to make porcelain, to invent enamel, and to *make glass.*"—*North American Review, Dec. 1880.*

Animals in Use   "One of the objections set forth against
Among   the Book of Mormon for several years, was
the Jaredites.   its reference to horses and cattle in use
among the ancient inhabitants of this continent. As M. Charnay observes in his contribution to the December *North American Review*, 'It is generally agreed that previous to the conquest there were neither oxen nor horses in America.' But on the landing of Lehi and his family upon this great country, Nephi states:

" 'And it came to pass that we did find upon the land of promise as we journeyed in the wilderness, that there were beasts in the forest of every kind, both the cow and the ox, and the ass and the horse, and the goat and the wild goat, and all manners of wild animals which were for the use of men.' (Book of Mormon p. 47.)

"But it also appears that these and other animals were in use on this land several centuries before the arrival of Lehi. For the colonists who settled here shortly after the dispersion from Babel and who are called the Jaredites, became rich in flocks and herds, as we read in the Book of Ether:

" ' Having all manner of fruit, and of grain, and of silks, and of fine linen, and of gold and of silver, and of precious things. And also all manner of cattle, of oxen, and cows, and of sheep and of swine, and of goats and also many other animals which were useful for the food of man; aud they also had horses and asses and there were elephants and cureloms and cumoms.' (Ibid p. 590.)

"In consequence of these and similar allusions in the Book of Mormon to animals which science, with quite as much arrogance as it complains of in theology, has pronounced unknown to American antiquity, the Book which gives the only clue to the ancient history of this continent has been repeatedly denounced as 'a clumsy imposture.'

"But the recent discoveries of Professor Marsh demonstrate the existence of cattle and horses and also of the elephant, the mastodion, the megatherium and other peculiar mammoth animals, which we have no doubt were anciently named as related in the above quotation from Ether. And now Charnay, puzzled and astonished, finds in the ruins of Tula, sixty-five miles north of the City of Mexico, animal remains which upset the dogmas of the scientists and corroborate the conclusions of Marsh as well as the statements in the Book of Mormon. Charnay says:

" ' Aug. 18.—We collected a few ornaments, also some animal remains, viz., some ribs (probably of the roebuck, though on this point I will not be positive, not being a geologist,) some small scapulas, two teeth, and stranger still, two enormous humeruses much larger than the humeruses of the ox; both of these bones are broken longitudinally, as though to take out the marrow. We found also the radius of an animal considerably larger than the horse.'

" 'Aug. 20.—In another edifice there were found some bones, among them the gigantic tibia of a ruminant, with the perineum attached. Could the animal have been a bison?'

" ' Aug. 21.—Here are the remains of unknown animals, probably of mammoth bisons domesticated by the Toltecs, at least used by them for food. This is the contradiction of history, which affirms that the Indians had no large domestic animals.'

" ' Aug. 24.—We are continually meeting with enigmas amid these ruins. Today I discovered a sheep's head in terra cotta.'

" 'Sept. 9.—I cannot but recognize among the many bones found in the progress of the work, jawbones of swine, sheep, and, as I believe, of oxen and horses.'

" The puzzled explorer, depending on the dictum of the scientists, came to the conclusion that these and many works of art which he unearthed, must have been left among the ancient ruins by a modern race, perhaps the Spaniards. But he took some specimens to the City of Mexico, and says :

" ' Senor del Cartillo, Professor of Zoology in the School of

Mines, on examining the bones found at Tula, pronounce them to be the remains of *Bos Americanus*, horse, Andes sheep, llama, stag, etc., and *fossil!* If his judgment is confirmed by the *savants* of Paris and the Smithsonian Institution, a new horizon is opened for the history of man in America. My victory will then be complete, as I shall have brought to light a new people, and a city unique in its originality, and shall have opened to the learned a new branch of natural history.'"—*Deseret Weekly News, Vol. xxix, p. 710.*

"Recent discoveries in the fossil beds of the Bad Lands of Nebraska prove that the horse originated in America.—*Atlantis, p. 54.*

"We find in America numerous representations of the elephant. * * * There are in Wisconsin a number of mounds of earth representing different animals—men, birds, and quadrupeds. Among the latter is a mound representing an elephant, 'so perfect in its proportions, and complete in its representation of an elephant, that its builders must have been well acquainted with all the physical characteristics of the animal which they delineated.' * * * On a farm in Louisa County, Iowa, a pipe was ploughed up which also represents an elephant. * * * It was found in a section where the ancient mounds were very abundant and rich in relics. The pipe is of sandstone, of the ordinary Mound-Builder's type, and has every appearance of age and usage. There can be no doubt of its genuineness. The finder had no conception of its archæological value.

"In the ruined city of Palenque we find, in one of the palaces, a stucco bass-relief of a priest. His elaborate head-dress or helmet represent very faithfully the head of an elephant. * * * The decoration known as 'elephant-trunks' is found in many parts of the ancient ruins of Central America, projecting from above the door-ways of the buildings.

"In Tylor's 'Researches into the Early History of Mankind,' p. 313, I find a remarkable representation of an elephan, taken from an ancient Mexican manuscript."—*Ibid, 168, 169, 170.*

Accounts "According to 'Popol Vuh,' the world had a be-
of the ginning.   There was a time when it did not exist.
Creation. Only 'Heaven' existed, below which all space was
an empty, silent, unchanging solitude.   Nothing existed there,
neither man, nor animal, nor earth nor tree.   Then appeared a
vast expanse of water on which divine beings moved in bright-
ness. 'They said earth!' and instantly the earth was created.
It came into being like a vapor; mountains rose above the
waters like lobsters, and were made.   Thus was the earth created by the Heart of Heaven.   Next came the creation of animals; but the gods were disappointed because the animals could
neither tell names, nor worship the Heart of Heaven.   Therefore it was resolved that man should be created.   First man
was made of earth, but his flesh had no cohesion; he was inert,
could not turn his head, and had no mind, although he could
speak; therefore he was consumed in the water.   Next men
were made of wood, and these multiplied, but they had neither
heart nor intellect, and could not worship, and so they withered
up and disappeared in the waters.   A third attempt followed.
Man was made of a tree called Tzite, and woman of the pith
of a reed; but these failed to think, speak or worship, and were
destroyed, all save a remnant, which still exists as a race of
small monkeys found in the forests.   A fourth attempt to create
the human race was successful, but the circumstances attending
this creation are veiled in mystery.   It took place before the
beginning of dawn, when neither sun nor moon had risen, and
it was a wonder-work of the Heart of Heaven.   Four men
were created, and they could reason, speak and see in such a
manner as to know all things at once.   They worshipped the
Creator with thanks for existence, but the gods, dismayed and
scared, breathed clouds on their eyes to limit their vision,
and cause them to be men and not gods.   Afterwards, while
the four men were asleep, the gods made for them beautiful
wives, and from these came all the tribes and families of the
earth."—"*Ancient America*," (*Baldwin*) *pp. 194-5.*

Bancroft, (vol. iii), says: "In the order of the Quichi creation, the heavens were first formed and their boundaries fixed by the Creator and Former, by whom all move and breathe, by whom all nations enjoy their wisdom and civilization. At first there was no man, or animal, or bird, or fish, or green herb— nothing but the firmament existed, the face of the earth was not yet to be seen, only the peaceful sea and the whole expanse of heaven. Silence pervaded all; not even the sea murmured; there was nothing but immobility and silence in the darkness —in the night. The Creator, the Former, the Dominator—the feathered Serpent—those that engender, those that give being, moved upon the water as a glowing light. Their name is Gucumatz, the Heart of Heaven God.''

"The persons of the Godhead having counseled regarding the creation of more perfect man, on the fourth attempt succeeded so that 'Verily, at last, were there found men worthy of their origin and their destiny; verily, at last, did the gods look upon beings who could see with their eyes and handle with their hands and understand with their hearts; grand of countenance and broad of limb, the four lives of our race stood up under the white rays of the morning star—sole light as yet of the primeval world—stood up and looked. Their great clear eyes swept rapidly over all; they saw the woods and rocks, the lakes and the sea, the mountains and the valleys, and the heavens that were above all; and they comprehended all and admired exceedingly. Then they returned thanks to those who had made the world, and all therein was: we offer up our thanks, twice— yea, verily thrice; we have received life, we speak, we walk, we taste, we hear and understand, we know both that which is near and that which is far off, we see all things, great and small, in all the heaven and earth. Thanks, then, Maker and Former, Father and Mother of our life, we have been created, we are.' ''

Legends of the Deluge. " It is a very remarkable fact,'' says Alfred Maury, "that we find in America traditions of the Deluge coming indefinitely nearer to that of the Bible and the Chaldean religion than among any people of the Old World.''

"The most important among the American traditions are the Mexican, for they appear to have been definitively fixed by symbol'c and mnemonic paintings before any contact with Europeans. According to these documents, the Noah of the Mexican cataclysm was Coxcox, called by certain peoples Teocipactli or Tezpi. He had saved himself, together with his wife Xochiquetzal, in a bark, or, according to other traditions, on a raft made of cypress-wood (*Cupressus disticha*). Paintings retracing the deluge of Coxcox have been discovered among the Aztecs, Miztecs, Zapotecs, Tlascaltecs, and Mechoacaneses. The tradition of the latter is still more strikingly in conformity with the story as we have it in Genesis, and in Chaldean sources. It tells how Tezpi embarked in a spacious vessel with his wife, his children, and several animals, and grain, whose preservation was essential to the subsistence of the human race. When the great god Tezcatlipoca decreed that the waters should retire, Tezpi sent a vulture from the bark. The bird, feeding on the carcasses with which the earth was laden, did not return. Tezpi sent out other birds, of which the humming-bird only came back with a leafy branch in its beak. Then Tezpi, seeing that the country began to vegetate, left his bark on the mountain of Colhuacan.

"The document, however, that gives the most valuable information," says Lenormant, "as to the cosmogony of the Mexicans is one known as 'Codex Vaticanus,' from the library where it is preserved. It consists of four symbolic pictures, representing the four ages of the world preceding the actual one. They were copied at Chobula from a manuscript anterior to the conquest, and accompanied by the explanatory commentary of Pedro de los Rios, a Dominican monk, who, in 1566, less than fifty years after the arrival of Cortez, devoted himself to the research of indigenous traditions as being necessary to his missionary work."—*See Atlantis p. 99.*

"It is found in the histories of the Toltecs that this age and *first world*, as they call it, lasted 1716 years; that men were destroyed by tremendous rains and lightning from the sky, and even all the land, without the exception of anything, and the highest mountains, were covered up and submerged in water *fifteen cubits* (caxtolmolatli); and here they added other fables of how men came to multiply from the few who escaped from this destruction in a 'toptlipetlocali;' that this word nearly signifies a close chest; and how, after men had multiplied, they erected a very high 'zacuali,' which is today a tower of great height, in order to take refuge in it should the second world (age) be destroyed. Presently their languages were confused, and, not being able to understand each other, they went to different parts of the earth."—"*Ixtlilxochitl Relaciones,*" *in Kingsborough's "Mex. Ant.," Vol. ix, p. 321.*

The following tradition was current among the Indians of the Great Lakes:

"In former times the father of the Indian tribes dwelt *toward the rising sun.* Having been warned in a dream that a deluge was coming upon the earth, he built a raft, on which he saved himself, with his family and all the animals. He floated thus for several months. The animals, who at that time spoke, loudly complained and murmured against him. At last a new earth appeared, on which he landed with all the animals, who from that time lost the power of speech, as a punishment for their murmurs against their deliverer."

Lehi and His People.   "In the first year of the reign of Zedekiah, king of Judah (B. C. 600), the Lord gave Lehi," (a Hebrew prophet, of the tribe of Manasseh,) "a number of prophetic dreams and visions, and, in compliance with the admonitions of those manifestations, he went forth among the Jews proclaiming the sorrows that would inevitably be theirs if they did not repent and return to the Lord. But the Jews treated Lehi just as they were treating all the rest of the prophets who came to them. They paid no heed to the message he bore. * * * But he did not cease to labor in their midst until their anger grew so intense that they sought his life; and they would have slain him if the Lord had not protected him; for it was not to be that Lehi should fall a victim to their hatred. The Lord had designed him for a greater work—he was to be the father of a multitude of people, and to this end God delivered him from the fury of the Jews. When it became impossible for him to remain longer and minister unto them, he was instructed to gather up such things as he could carry and take them into the wilderness with his family, where the Lord would teach him what more He required at his hands.

"When Lehi received the command to depart, he immediately set about fulfilling it, and taking with him his family and such goods and food as he could carry, he left the doomed city, where he had so long dwelt, leaving behind him his house and property, his gold, his silver and other precious things, all ot which he willingly gave up that he might be obedient to the heavenly message.

"Lehi's family consisted of his wife, Sariah, and his four sons, Laman, Lemuel, Sam and Nephi. Lehi had also daughters, but whether they were born at this time is not evident from the record. We have no account in the Book of Mormon of the precise road which Lehi and his family took when they left Jerusalem. Undoubtedly they traveled through the wilderness of Judea southward till they reached the eastern arm of the Red Sea.

*　　*　　*　　*　　*　　*　　*　　*

"When the people of Lehi reached the sea shore they rejoiced greatly that their tedious wanderings were over. Nephi, by Divine direction, built a ship to carry them across these great waters. When the vessel was finished, the voice of the Lord came to Lehi, commanding that he and his people should arise and go aboard the ship. The next day they embarked, every one according to his age, taking with them their provisions, seeds, and such other things as it was desirable they should carry across the ocean to their new home, far away on its opposite shores."—*Dictionary of the Book of Mormon*, *213, 214, 216.*

Peruvian History and the Book of Mormon. "'According to Montesinos,' says Baldwin, 'there were three distinct periods in the history of Peru. First, there was a period which began with the origin of civilization, and lasted until the first or second century of the Christian era. Second, there was a period of disintegration, decline and disorder, introduced by successful invasions from the east and southeast, during which the country was broken up into small states, and many of the arts of civilization were lost ; this period lasted more than a thousand years. Third and last came the period of the Incas, who revived civilization and restored the empire. He discards the wonder stories told of Manco-Copac and Mama-Ocllo, and gives the Peruvian nation a beginning which is, at least, not incredible. It was originated, he says, by a people led by FOUR BROTHERS, who settled in the valley of Cuzco, and developed civilization there in a very human way. The YOUNGEST OF THESE BROTHERS ASSUMED SUPREME AUTHORITY AND BECAME THE FIRST OF A LONG LINE OF SOVEREIGNS.

"Those who are familiar with the Book of Mormon, understand that the Nephite colony from Palestine landed in South America and that when their descendents moved northward they found the north land covered with the remnants of an ancient race, with their mounds, monuments and ruined cities spread over the face of the land. In this colony were Laman, Lemuel, Sam and Nephi, four brothers, of whom Nephi was the youngest and who became their leader and the first of a line of rulers. These brothers divided in consequence of the rebellion and wickedness of Laman and Lemuel, and the darkness of skin that came upon their posterity was a curse from the Lord for their iniquity. They became that ruthless race that eventually stamped out the civilized Nephites, in consequence of the latter falling into transgression."—*Deseret Weekly News, Vol. xxix, p. 262.*

The Compass. "And it came to pass after they had loosed me, behold, I took the compass, and it did work whither I desired it. And it came to pass that I prayed unto the Lord;

and after I had prayed, the winds did cease, and the storm did cease, and there was a great calm."—*I. Nephi xviii: 21.*

"I find in the 'Report of United States Explorations for a Route for a Pacific Railroad,' a description of a New Mexican Indian priest, who foretells the result of a proposed war by placing a piece of wood in a bowl of water, and causing it to turn to the right or left, or sink or rise, as he directs it. This is incomprehensible, unless the wood, like the ancient Chinese compass, contained a piece of magnetic iron hidden in it, which would be attracted or repulsed, or even drawn downward, by a piece of iron held in the hand of the priest, on the outside of the bowl. If so, this trick was a remembrance of the mariner's compass transmitted from age to age by the medicine men. The reclining statue of Chac-Mol, of Central America, holds a bowl or dish upon its breast, * * * The Etruscans set their temples squarely with the cardinal points of the compass; so did the Egytians, the Mexicans, and *the Mound Builders of America.* Could they have done this without the magnetic compass?"—*Atlantis pp. 445, 446.*

The Aborigines of America Were of the Same Origin. "Mr. Bradford in his researches into the origin of the red race, adopts the following conclusions in regard to the ancient occupants of North America:

"That they were all of the same origin, branches of the same race, and possessed of similar customs and institutions.

"That they were populous and occupied a great extent of territory.

"That they had arrived at a considerable degree of civilization, were associated in large communities and lived in extensive cities.

"That they possessed the use of many of the metals, such as lead, copper, gold, and silver, and probably the art of working in them,

"That they sculptured in stone and sometimes used that material in the construction of their edifices.

"That they had the knowledge of the arch of receding steps; of the art of pottery, producing urns and utensils formed with taste and constructed upon the principles of chemical composition; and the art of brick-making.

"That they worked the salt springs, and manufactured salt.

"That they were an agricultural people, living under the influence and protection of regular forms of governments.

"That they possessed a decided system of religion, and a mythology connected with astronomy, which, with its sister science, geometry, was in the hands of the priesthood.

" That they were skilled in the art of of fortification.

"That the epoch of their original settlement in the United States is of great antiquity; and

"That the only indications of their origin to be gathered from the locality of their ruined monuments, point toward Mexico.

"Mr. Lewis H. Morgan finds evidence that the American aborgines had a common origin in what he calls 'their system of consanguinity and affinity.' He says, ' The Indian nations from the Atlantic to the Rocky Mountains and from the Arctic sea to the Gulf of Mexico, with the exception of the Esquimaux, have the same system. It is elaborate and complicated in its general form and details; and while deviations from uniformity occur in the systems of different stocks, the radical feaures are in the main constant. This identity in the essential characteristics of a system so remarkable tends to show that it must have been transmitted with the blood to each stock from a common original source. It affords the strongest evidence yet obtained of unity in origin of the Indian nations within the region defined.' "—*Baldwin's "Ancient America," page 56.*

Law of Moses Kept by the Nephites. "And notwithstanding we believe in Christ, we keep the law of Moses, and look forward with steadfastness unto Christ, until the law shall be fulfilled."—*II Nephi xxv: 24.*

A Stone Found on which the Ten Commandments were Engraved. "Between 1860 and 1865, four different stones with Hebrew inscriptions upon them were found in Licking County, Ohio, though not all in the same neighborhood. * * * The fourth stone is the most remarkable of all. There was an extended series of Indian mounds, fortifications, and enclosures around Newark. One of the most remarkable was an enormous stone mound of conical form, eight miles south of the spot where Newark now stands. It is believed that some thousands of loads of stones were taken from it for the Ohio canal and other purposes. It was once five hundred and eighty feet in circumference at the base, and forty to fifty feet high. An impression grew among the workmen that there was a circle of little mounds of pure clay, enclosed within the great mound, and standing round near the periphery at the base. In the removal of one of these clay mounds, a piece of wood was found like the shell of an old log, and on it several copper rings were lying. A further examination decided that this piece of wood was only the covering of a lower piece, which had the form of a large trough, and the whole of its interior seemed to have been once lined with a very coarse cloth, so rotten that a piece as large as a thumb nail could not be held together. This trough contained several human bones, a lock of very fine black hair, about six or eight inches long, and ten more copper rings. It was farther found that this coffin lay in a two feet thick bed of very tough fire clay of the color of putty. In digging into this fire clay, a stone box was struck in its lower part. The box was drawn out with care, was found to be of a rounded, oblong shape, and in color, lighter than copper. Its two halves were cemented together. After considerable effort, the cement was broken, and the two halves separated, and in the center of the box was a stone, on which the Ten Commandments were engraved. Now, keep these facts in their connection: the stone lodged in the center of the stone box; this box buried in a stratum of fire clay; above the box the coffin also lodged in the fire clay; the clay mound and then the enormous stone mound covering all.

"The stone has for its length about six inches and seven-eighths; for its width, about two inches and seven-eighths, and for its thickness, about one inch and five-eighths. On one side the greater part of the surface is depressed, and a carved human figure is in this depression. On the other side the central surface is a protruded plane, but the protrusion on one side does not correspond exactly with the depression on the other side. The human figure stands out in relief on the depressed plane; it has the appearance of a noble man, dressed in the robes of the Priesthood, and over his head, written in Hebrew, is the name Moses. At the feet of the image there is an empty space through the stone, and then a round handle is united to the main stone at its ends, as if the stone was once carried by a strap passed through this empty space. On the back and on the sides and top are engraved in Hebrew characters (though inferior to those on the other stones) the Ten Commandments. Not exactly as we have the Ten Commandments in the Bible, but somewhat abridged for want of room; and there is a peculiarity about them—they are not written underneath one another, but in different directions. The Commandments, though not here given at full length, contain all the essential points; that is to say, when you come to the one: 'Thou shalt not take the name of the Lord thy God in vain,' that is all there is of it. The second clause is not included; but all the Ten Commandments are there. We may here ask: Who, but a people acquainted with the dealings of the Lord with the House of Israel, could have prepared such a stone as this—*Geo. Reynolds in Contributor, Vol. xvii, pp. 233-4.*

Practices Among the Lamanites —Circumcision. Lord Kingsbury tells us the Central Americans practiced circumcision, and McKenzie (quoted by Ritzius) says he saw the ceremony performed by the Chippeways.

Sacrifices. "The Peruvians, when they sacrificed animals, examined their entrails, and from these prognosticated the future."—*Atlantis p. 144.*

Baptism. "The use of confession and penace was known in the religious ceremonies of some of the American nations. Baptism was a religious ceremony with them, and the bodies of the dead were sprinkled with water."—*Atlantis p. 144.*

Eclipse at the Death of Christ. "And it came to pass that there was thick darkness upon all the face of the land, insomuch, that the inhabitants thereof who had not fallen, could feel the vapor of darkness. * * * And it came to pass that it did last for the space of three days, that there was no light seen; and there was great mourning, and howling, and weeping among all the people continually; yea, great were the groanings of the people, because of the darkness and the great destruction which had come upon them."—*III Nephi viii: 20, 23.*

Boturini says that the eclipse of the sun, which happened at the death of our Savior, was marked in their paintings in the year 7. Tochtli, and that some learned Spaniards have compared their chronology with ours, and have found that they reckoned from the creation to the birth of Christ 5,199 years, which corresponds with the Roman calendar.

Clavigero says: "Upon reading Boturini, I set about comparing the Toltecan years with ours, and I found the thirty-fourth year of Christ, or the thirtieth of our era, to be the 7. Tochtli."

Christ's Visit to the Nephites. "And it came to pass as they understood, they cast their eyes up again towards heaven; and behold, they saw a man descending out of heaven; and he was clothed in a white robe, and he came down and stood in the midst of them, and the eyes of the whole multitude were turned upon him, and they durst not open their mouths, even one to another, and wist not what it meant, for they thought it was an angel that had appeared unto them. And it came to pass, that he stretched forth his hand and spake unto the people, saying, Behold, I am Jesus Christ, whom the prophets testified shall come into the world."—*III. Nephi xi: 8-10.*

"*From the distant East,* from the fabulous Hue Hue Tlapalan, this mysterious person came to Tula, and became the patron god and high-priest of the ancestors of the Toltecs. He is described as having been *a white man*, with strong formation of body, broad forehead, large eyes, and *flowing beard*. He wore a mitre on his head, and was dressed in a LONG WHITE ROBE reaching to his feet, and covered with red crosses. In his hand he held a sickle. His habits were ascetic, he never married, was most chaste and pure in life, and is said to have endured penace in a neighboring mountain, not for its effects upon himself, but as a warning to others. He condemned sacrifices, except of fruits and flowers, and was known as the god of peace; for, when addressed on the subject of war, he is reported to have stopped his ears with his fingers."—"*North Amer. of Antiq.*," *p. 268.*

Records Kept by the Nephites. "And it come o pass that the Lord commanded me, wherefore I did make plates of ore, that I might engraven upon them the record of my people. And upon the plates which I made, I did engraven the record of my father, and also our journeyings in the wilderness, and the prophecies of my father: and also many of mine own prophecies have I engraven upon them."—*I Nephi xix: 1.*

Relics of the Mound Builders. "At the annual meeting of the Davenport (Iowa) Academy of Natural Sciences, the President read a very interesting report of the progress of the institution, in which extended notice was given to the subject of the Mound Builders of the Mississippi Valley. The address shows that they were a numerous and industrious people, altogether different from the present race of American Indians, and occupying the country in much earlier times than the latter; that they were of different tribes, but domestic in their habits; that they lived in a very simple manner, possessed few mechanical contrivances, but were a laborious, painstaking people; that they had some system of barter with neighboring tribes, as shown by the occurrence in the mounds of large sea shells, which, the reader opined, must have come from the Gulf

of Mexico; obsidian which must have come from the Far West;
mica, not to be found in this region; galena, etc.

"It appears, too, that they smoked tobacco, not merely for
pleasure, but as a ceremonial observance, for the pipes discovered are, in many instances, very elaborately and beautifully
carved out of a great variety of kinds of stone, generally of a
rather soft character, and were apparently held in very high es-
timation, perhaps almost sacred.

"The report says: *   *   *   *   *   *   *   *

"'Strangest of all, and most contrary to the opinion of all
archæologists hitherto, it now appears that *the Mound Builders
had a written language.* Whence derived or what its origin, is
matter of the merest conjecture. What its affinities, or whether
any connection with other written languages—ancient or modern—no one has, as yet, been able to determine.

"'The inscribed tablets in our museum—the only ones of
much significance or importance perhaps, which have as yet
been discovered in the mounds—have attracted much attention,
both in this country and in Europe, and by all eminent and
well-informed archæologists, are considered of the highest
importance. They are certain to stimulate research, which will
doubtless lead to further discoveries, until it may well be hoped
that the key to the language may ultimately be discovered, and
something of a history of this ancient people may be made out
as written by themselves.

"'Whether the language was understood by all, or only by a
more learned few, or whether the tablets were heirlooms and
cherished relics, cannot now be scarcely even guessed.

"'A rather significant circumstance, perhaps, is the fact that
in the same mound with the two tablets first found were the
bones of a young child, partially preserved by the contact of
a large number—about 300—copper beads, indicating it to be
an important personage, and that persons of high n k were
buried there.

"'Some doubts of course have been expressed regarding the
genuineness of the tablets, though not to any great extent by

competent and candid archæologists, and we feel no uneasiness on that account.

"'The tablets have been sent to the Smithsonian Institute for examination, and were retained there and subjected to the most thorough scrutiny for two months, during which time the National Academy of Sciences held its meeting there, and the heliotype plates of them were obtained under the directions of Prof. Baird himself. They were also exhibited throughout the sessions of the meetings of the American Association for the Advancement of Science at Boston, last August.

"'Any author, or other person, who cared to inform himself of the facts, has and has always had ample opportunity to do so, and would at once see that the circumstances of the finding were such as utterly to preclude all possibility of fraud or imposition.

"'The evidence that they are coeval with the other relics that is, that they were inhumed with them, and before the mound was built, is ample and conclusive, and will be so considered by any unbiased man.

"'No pre-historic relic ever found has better evidence to establish its genuineness than these, and not one suspicious circumstance in connection with them has been pointed out, nor can there be.

"'We shall confidently hope for and gladly welcome further discoveries by whomsoever made, tending to throw more light upon this still obscure and intensely interesting problem, of our earliest predecessors on this continent.

"'Our collections of mound relics now consists of the four inscribed tablets, thirty-two mound builder's pipes, twenty-five copper axes, three hundred copper beads, fourteen copper awls, and a great number and variety of other relics from the mounds of this region, constituting the most extensive, rare and unique collection of its kind in this country, and probably in the world. Besides these, this department contains two hundred and twenty-five vessels of ancient pottery, over one thousand stone implements, and ten thousand of flint, besides about an equal number of broken ones and fragments worth preserving.'

BANCROFT

" This evidence is valuable, as it is conclusive that the pre-historic inhabitants of this country did, as described in the Book of Mormon, make records in a language which, through changes and admixtures, was different from others.''—*Millenial Star Vol. xliii, pp. 132, 133.*

Records Hid in the Hill Cumorah. " And it came to pass that when we had gathered in all our people in one to the land of Cumorah, behold I, Mormon, began to be old; and knowing it to be the last struggle of my people, and having been commanded of the Lord that I should not suffer that the records which had been handed down by our fathers, which were sacred, to fall into the hands of the Lamanites, (for the Lamanites would destroy them, therefore I made this record out of the plates of Nephi, and hid up in the hill Cumorah, all the records which had been entrusted to me by the hand of the Lord, save it were these few plates which I gave unto my son Moroni."—*Mormon vi: 6.*

Prophecies— Truth to Spring Out of the Earth. "Truth shall spring out of the earth; and righteousness shall look down from heaven.—*Psal. lxxxv: 11.*

" Drop down, ye heavens, from above, and let the skies pour down righteousness: let the earth open, and let them bring forth salvation, and let righteousness spring up together; I, the Lord, have created it.—*Isa. xlv: 8.*

" And thou shalt be brought down, and shalt speak out of the ground, and thy speech shall be low out of the dust, and thy voice shall be, as of one that hath a familiar spirit, out of the ground, and thy speech shall whisper out of the dust."—*Isa. xxix: 4.*

Traditions Among the Lamanites. "We shall now introduce some circumstantial evidence, from American Antiquities, and from the traditions of the natives:
" ' First, says Mr. Boudinot, 'it is said among their principal or beloved men, that they have it handed down from their ancestors, that the Book which the white people have was once

theirs; that while they had it they prospered exceedingly, &c. They also say, that their fathers were possessed of an extraordinary Divine Spirit, by which they foretold future events, and contrólled the common course of nature; and this they transmitted to their offspring, on condition of their obeying the sacred laws; that they did, by these means, bring down showers of blessings upon their beloved people; but that this power, for a long time past, has entirely ceased ' Colonel James Smith in his Journal, while a prisoner among the natives, says, 'They have a tradition, that in the beginning of this continent the angels, or heavenly inhabitants, as they call them, frequently visited the people, and talked with their forefathers, and gave directions how to pray.'   *   *   *   There is a tradition related by an aged Indian, of the Stockbridge tribe, that their fathers were once in possession of a 'Sacred Book,' which was handed down from generation to generation ; and at last hid in the earth, since which time they had been under the feet of their enemies.   But these oracles were to be restored to them again; and *then* they would triumph over their enemies, and regain their rights and privileges.   Mr. Boudinot, after recording many traditions similar to the above, at length remarks: ' Can any man read this short account of Indian traditions, drawn from tribes of various nations, from the west to the east, and from the south to the north, wholly separated from each other, written by different authors of the best character, both for knowledge and integrity, possessing the best means of information, at various and distant times, without any possible communication with each other; and yet suppose that all this is the effect of chance, accident, or design, from a love of the marvellous. or a premeditated intention of deceiving, and thereby ruining their well-established reputation?' "—*Voice of Warning pp. 129, 130.*

Nephite Records Found by Joseph Smith. "The Book of Mormon claims to be the sacred history of ancient America, written by a succession of ancient prophets, who inhabited that vast continent.   The plates of gold, containing

this history, were discovered by a young man, named Joseph
Smith, through the ministry of a holy angel on the evening
and morning of the 21st and 22nd of September, A. D. 1823.
Four years after their discovery, or on the morning of the 22nd
of September, 1827, the angel of the Lord permitted Mr. Smith
to take these sacred records from the place of their deposit.
The hill in which they were found buried, is situated in the
town of Manchester, Ontario County, State of New York. With
the plates were also found a Urim and Thummim. Each plate
was not far from seven by eight inches in width and length,
being not quite as thick as common tin. Each was filled on
both sides with engraved Egyptian characters; and the whole
were bound together in a volume, as the leaves of a book, and
fastened at one edge with three rings running through each.
This volume was something near six inches in thickness, a part
of which was sealed. The characters or letters upon the un-
sealed part were small and beautifully engraved. Mr. Smith,
through the aid of the Urim and Thummim, and by the gift and
power of God, translated this record into the English language.
This translation contains about the same amount of reading as
the Old Testament. A large edition of this wonderful book
was first published early in 1830."—*Orson Pratt's Works,
pp. 221-222.*

A Prophecy   "And the vision of all is become unto you as
and its   the words of a book that is sealed, which men
Fulfillment. deliver to one that is learned, saying, Read
this, I pray thee: and he saith, I cannot; for it is sealed:

"And the book is delivered to him that is not learned, saying,
Read this, I pray thee: and he saith, I am not learned.—*Isaiah
xxix: 11, 12.*

"After obtaining the Book of Mormon, through the ministry
of the angel, 'out of the ground,' Mr. Smith transcribed some
of the original characters upon paper, and sent them by the
hands of Martin Harris, a farmer, to the city of New York,
where they were presented to Professor Anthon, a man deeply

learned in both ancient and modern languages. Mr. Harris very anxiously requested him to read it, but he replied that he could not. None of the learned have as yet been able to decipher the characters and hieroglyphics which are found among the ancient ruins, in almost every part of America. The written language of ancient America is a sealed language to this generation. In the year 1841, Professor Anthon wrote a letter to an Episcopal minister, in New Rochelle, Westchester County, near New York, in answer to an inquiry made by the minister in reference to the words or characters said to have been presented to him. Professor Anthon's letter was written with permission to publish; its avowed object being to put a stop to the spread of the fullness of the gospel, contained in the Book of Mormon. We here give a short extract from it, taken from a periodical, entitled *The Church Record*, (Vol. i., No. 22.)

"'Many years ago, the precise date I do not recollect, a plain-looking countryman called upon me with a letter from Dr Samuel L. Mitchell, requesting me to examine and give my opinion upon a certain paper, marked with various characters, which the Doctor confessed he could not decipher, and which the bearer of the note was very anxious to have explained.'

"Here, then, is the testimony of the learned, that a man did call upon him with 'the words of a book.' But the learned professor continues :

"'A very brief examination convinced me that it was a mere *hoax*, and a very clumsy one, too. The characters were arranged in columns, like the Chinese mode of writing, and presented the most singular medley that I ever beheld. Greek, Hebrew and all sorts of letters, more or less distorted, either through unskillfulness or from actual design, were intermingled with sundry delineations of half moons, stars and other natural objects, and the whole ended in a rude representation of the Mexican Zodiac.'

"Professor Anthon, no doubt thought that this statement would militate against the Book of Mormon; but we consider it a great acquisition of evidence, confirmatory of the truth of that book, when compared with the discoveries of the

glyphs and characters among the ancient ruins of America.
The celebrated antiquarian, Professor Rafinesque, in speaking of
the glyphs discovered on the ruins of a stone city found in
Mexico, says:

"'The glyphs of Otolum are written from top to bottom, like
the *Chinese*, or from side to side, indifferently, like the *Egyptian*, and Demotic Lybian. Although the most common way
of writing the groups is in rows, and each group separated, yet
we find some formed, as it were, in oblong squares or tablets,
like those of *Egypt.—Orson Pratt's Works, pp. 295-6.*

Mexican "We have recently had the opportunity of exam-
Calendar ining a photograph of the wonderful Calendar
Stone.   Stone of the ancient Mexicans.. Elder Moses
Thatcher brought with him from the city of Mexico some stere-
oscopic views of that remarkable relic of antiquity. A work
has been published by Harper & Bros., of New York, written by
J. T. Short, Esq., and entitled 'The North Americans of Antiq-
uity,' which contains many items of interest to the Latter-day
Saints, and among them a description and explanation of the
Mexican Calendar Stone, which unwittingly corroborates the
Book of Mormon. The author opposes the idea of the Israel-
itish origin of the American Indians, and ridicules the Book of
Mormon, but his work contains many things confirmatory of the
sacred record which was brought forth from the Hill of Cu-
morah, under the guidance of divine revelation.

"The Calendar Stone of the ancient Mexicans, with other
relics, was, in December, 1790, dug up in the Plaza Major of the
City of Mexico, and is now built into the wall of the Cathedral
of that City, where it can be seen by passers by. It is a rectan-
gular block of porphyry, thirteen feet one inch square, of the
enormous estimated weight of twenty-four tons. Its face is
most elaborately carved with geometrical precision, as recog-
nized by Humboldt and others, and its symbols and hieroglyphics have been deciphered by the learned. It is found to be a
calendar of the ancient people of Mexico, with the days,
months, years, cycles, etc., and other information such as is
generally associated with such works, recorded thereon.

"Without an engraving it would be more likely to confuse the reader than otherwise if an attempt were here made to explain its multitudinous hieroglyphics. It is the outside circles of these symbols, only, which now claim our attention. In this is represented the national cycle of fifty-two years. With regard to it Mr. Short remarks (page 458):

"'To return to Prof. Valentine's investigations, it will be observed that there are twenty-four of the cycle symbols, two of which are nearly hidden under the helm plumes. The product of twenty-four and fifty-two gives us a period of 1,248 years. But what have we to do with this result? The triangular shaped figures which point to the central tablet cut at the top of the stone, indicate that we must make a calculation and it remains for us to interpret the symbol. It is recognizable as the sign Acatl accompanied by the number thirteen; a year, which, according to the authentic tables of reduction, corresponds to the year 1479, A. D.; a date which is confirmed as being the year in which the Calendar Stone was finished and set up in the great pyramid of Mexico, by the statement of the native writer Tezozomoc, that its author, King Axaycatl, became ill from his exertions at the tragic celebrations of the completion of the temple and lived scarcely a year, at the same time fixing the date in 1480. If we subtract 1248 years from the known date 1479, A. D., we have the year 231 A. D.; a date which no doubt marks the beginning of the national era of the Nahuas and probably designates the year of their arrival in Mexico by the ports Tampeco, Xicalanco and Bacalar.'

"Now let us turn to the Book of Mormon and find what is there stated with regard to the year 'which no doubt marks the beginning of the national era of the Nahuas.' (A. D. 231.) But before we do so, we must remind our readers that from the time of the Savior's personal appearance on this continent to two hundred years after His birth at Bethlehem, an era of perfect unity, undisturbed peace and abounding righteousness, universally prevailed among the people who inhabited the vast continents of North and South America, also that from that date evil crept in, unity ceased and vice and crime gradually and unceasingly increased until the Nephite nation was destroyed. Now, let us listen to the inspired record; it states:

"'And now it came to pass in this year, yea, in the two hundred and thirty-first year, there was a great division among the people.

"'And it came to pass that in this year there arose a people who were called the Nephites, and they were true believers in Christ; and among them were those who were called by the Lamanites, Jacobites, and Josephites, and Zoramites;

"'Therefore the true believers in Christ, and the true worshippers of Christ, (among whom were the three disciples of Jesus who should tarry,) were called Nephites, and Jacobites, and Josephites, and Zoramites.

"'And it came to pass that they who rejected the gospel were called Lamanites, and Lemuelites, and Ishmaelites; and they did not dwindle in unbelief but they did wilfully rebel against the gospel of Christ; and they did teach their children that they should not believe, even as their fathers, from the beginning, did dwindle.

"'And it was because of the wickedness and abomination of their fathers, even as it was in the beginning. And they were taught to hate the children of God, even as the Lamanites were taught to hate the children of Nephi, from the beginning.'—B. of M. n. e. pp. 546-7.

"Can it possibly be claimed as a mere *coincidence* that the Nahua nation, one of the most important and in former years one of the strongest and most intelligent branches of the Lamanite race, should date the commencement of its national existence from the exact year of this great division of the people? Its historians would undoubtedly, as all nations are prone to do, date back their origin as a separate people as far as possible, to give the glamor of antiquity to their race; and thus we find them taking advantage of the very first opportunity and mingling their traditions with the authentic annals of the inspired historians. It is probable that other tribes and branches of the great Lamanite family, when they permanently settled down and commenced to build up kingdoms, dated their origin from this self-same date. Whilst this ancient Mexican calendar thus bears on its sculptured face undying testimony of the truth of the Book of Mormon, that holy book in its turn testifies to the exactness and accuracy of the Calendar."—*Deseret Weekly News Vol. xxix, p. 214.*